THE COMPLETE MODERN GUIDE TO BASEMENT WATERPROOFING

By J. Scott Gallawa

J. Scott Gallawa
9510 Hummingbird Blvd
Pensacola, Florida 32514

Got Questions?
Contact the Author: jsgallawa@cox.net

TABLE OF CONTENTS

TABLE OF CONTENTS (continued)

ILLUSTRATIONS

Note: Gravel is not depicted for clarity

FORWARD

Of all the situations that confront a homeowner, few can be as frustrating, mystifying and downright depressing as a leaking basement. Every year, millions of Americans nationwide experience the heartbreak of seeing their possessions ruined by water damage and their home's foundation compromised by water pressure. Keep the word "pressure" in mind. We'll refer back to it many times (hydrostatic pressure = "standing water" pressure).

This publication will summarize the reasons why basements leak and what up-to-date technology is available to handle the various problems. Oftentimes the homeowner can participate in the correction of foundation seepage. So, I have included a do-it-yourself section for the adventurous. However, if these solutions range beyond the scope of the reader, Chapter 7 offers practical recommendations that will facilitate the wise and prudent selection of a waterproofing contractor should your problem be severe enough to merit such action.

The author has over 30 years experience as a field technician and supervisor and has been involved with more than 15,000 homes, each undergoing varying degrees of water infiltration. He has determined the solution for foundation dampness, corrected basements that habitually flood and has dealt with and resolved everything in between. We are confident that this book will not only shed light on your problem, but will put you well on the road towards economically restoring your basement to a fresh, dry, enjoyable part of your home.

CHAPTER 1

How and Why Does My Basement Leak?

In order to understand what options exist for solving a water problem in your basement, you must first be familiar with some basic facts about foundation construction and the dynamics of water pressure. The illustrations in **Figure 1** and **Figure 2** depict side views of two different below-grade (below ground level) walls. I have selected a hollow cinder block wall and a solid poured concrete wall to illustrate the various elements making up the stages of basement seepage. Familiarize yourself with these drawings, as they will become the keystone in comprehending why your basement leaks and what to do about it.

WATER IS HEAVY!

Have you ever carried two five-gallon buckets filled with water? Well, guess what? Water is definitely heavy. During a soaking rainstorm or a rainstorm causing a snowmelt, thousands of pounds of water pressure are exerted against your basement walls and floor. This unfortunate situation is compounded because many homes are built on deposits of hardpan clay, which do not allow for speedy water percolation into the deeper subsoils. The result is that huge amounts of water pressure build up around your home. The question is, can your home resist the water's onslaught?

EDITORIAL

Most builders offer only a one-year warranty against basement seepage on new homes. And when an existing home is sold, most states require a one-year dry basement warranty. This shows that the various watch dog consumer agencies are well aware that basement seepage problems exist on a huge scale. Unfortunately, building techniques reflect the fact that homebuilders are not required to furnish a more comprehensive guarantee than the standard one year.

FIGURE 1 CINDER BLOCK WALL DETAIL

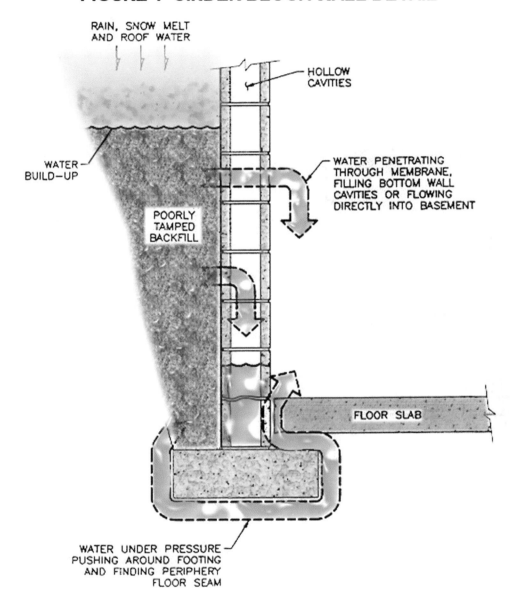

CINDER BLOCK

NOT TO SCALE

FIGURE 2   POURED CONCRETE WALL DETAIL

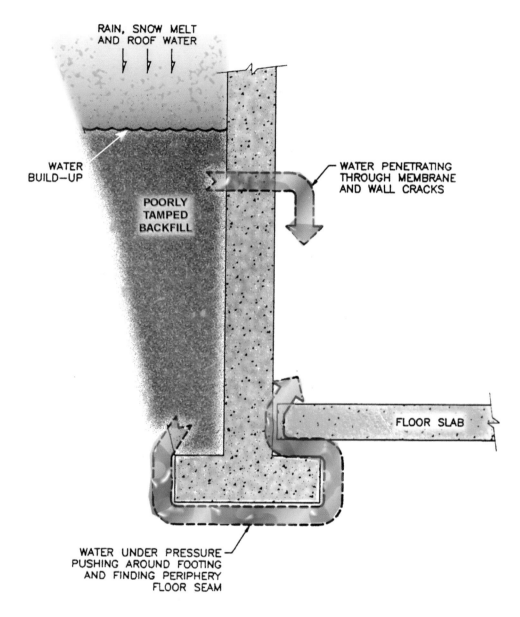

RAIN, SNOW MELT
AND ROOF WATER

WATER
BUILD—UP

POORLY
TAMPED
BACKFILL

WATER PENETRATING
THROUGH MEMBRANE
AND WALL CRACKS

FLOOR SLAB

WATER UNDER PRESSURE
PUSHING AROUND FOOTING
AND FINDING PERIPHERY
FLOOR SEAM

POURED CONCRETE

NOT TO SCALE

HYDROSTATIC PRESSURE = LEAKS

In order to gain a greater overview of a complex problem, let's look at how the average American basement gets built.

First of all, the contractor digs a hole in which to place the basement. Oftentimes this excavation takes place in dense, heavy clay that is typical of many areas in the Midwest, throughout the Northeast, Mid-Atlantic and Southeastern states. If it rains copiously during the excavation period and before the basement is built, one can see large amounts of water standing in the excavation hole because the rainwater cannot percolate downwards through the dense clay. If the excavation takes place in an area where springs are active, water can be observed gently running continuously into the excavation site from the sides of the hole, even in the absence of rainfall. Basements or crawlspaces are placed anywhere from 3 feet to 14 feet deep in the earth and the depths of excavations vary according to the architect's design. One thing is for sure, if the soil is of a type that type traps and holds water for longer than 48 hours, then the basement built there is in jeopardy of leaking unless properly waterproofed and drained. But, we'll get to that later.

After the space for the basement is fully excavated and is large enough to accommodate the basement as well as an additional six to seven feet working space beyond where the walls will stand, the footing is poured. The footing is the continuous ribbon of concrete on which the foundation walls will be placed. The structural integrity of this footing is extremely important because tons of foundation walls, plus the superstructure of the house will be permanently resting on it. If shortcuts are taken or if the footing is somehow "sub-code," then the chances that the basement will leak rise dramatically.

Once the footing is in and cured, the building of the walls begins. In modern times, the typical construction materials used for basement walls are cinder blocks, cement blocks or poured concrete. Sometimes they are combined on a single foundation. **Figures 1** and **2** show both a hollow wall and a solid wall. Cinder or cement blocks are laid one upon the other in a staggered and interlocking fashion, thereby creating a hollow, two-sided wall. The poured concrete wall is solid. The techniques used to solve water seepage problems affecting these two types of walls are quite different. Can you see some obvious differences with how the water enters the two types of walls? Hold those thoughts. They will be pertinent later.

After the walls are laid up, as in the case of cinder blocks, or poured into forms as with poured concrete, and they cure (or strengthen as the concrete becomes harder day by day), they are ready for the conventional waterproofing techniques of today.

With cinder or cement blocks, the builder parges on one coat of sandmix cement (1 part Portland cement and 2-½ parts builder's sand), sometimes two coats are used depending upon local codes. This coat of sandmix cement covers the entire surface of the wall, from the footing up to the ground level (grade level). Poured concrete doesn't require parging. By itself, this coating would still allow water to penetrate the wall by means of a natural action called capillarity. This is a large word simply meaning "wick action." Poured concrete and concrete products such as cement and cinder block cannot resist water penetration on their own. They are porous and absorb water like a sponge. Walls standing below grade are usually cementitious (made from cement products) and therefore require a waterproofing membrane placed over their exterior face in order to repel groundwater. This process of applying the waterproofing membrane is generally the weak link in the chain of construction steps that leads to so many water problems later in the life of the house.

THE MEMBRANE

Typically, the builder will spray or brush a very thin coat of liquid tar (and I mean thin, like the coat of paint on your car) on the walls once the cement coating has cured. The builder will then cover this thin asphalt membrane with a layer of plastic (6 mils) held onto the wall with a piece of furring strip tacked along the top of the wall at the grade level. Lamentably enough, this plastic, in my experience, goes on quite haphazardly. In many cases, as a result of construction mishaps, there are large rips and holes found in the plastic before the foundation is backfilled. This plastic should cover the surface of the below grade walls from bottom to top around the entire perimeter of the basement.

BACKFILLING

Before the foundation is backfilled, that is, before the dirt which came out of the excavation is bulldozed back around the house, filling in the area where the workmen stood, an inspection for rips in the plastic should take place. Unfortunately, this is not a common practice and even if it was, the next step in the construction process would negate such an inspection. What happens? Well, here's the rub—and it is a rub! Stones in the backfill soil are rubbing on and cutting the plastic, slashing through the paper thin tar membrane. That's right, these sharp-edged rocks (and any miscellaneous backfill material) are ripping the plastic and stripping areas of the wall of its tar membrane. This leaves the new wall beginning its life semi-defenseless against future water penetration. But that's not all!

As the bulldozer or backhoe pushes the excavated earth back around the newly built walls, something very important is happening—or not happening—depending upon your point of view. None of this soil is being tamped! Not one square foot is being compacted as it goes back. Obviously, the bulldozer or backhoe cannot maneuver into the backfill area until the soil has reached a close proximity to grade level, lest the heavy machine should tumble in.

As the soil reaches the level of the existing grade, the bulldozer can then come reasonably close to the foundation walls and let its weight press down upon the recently backfilled earth. Now, it may be assumed that this amount of compaction will duplicate the density of the soil prior to its being disturbed to make room for the basement. Wrong! What has occurred will affect the house for years to come. In all probability, only the top 4 to 5 feet of the 9 to 12 foot excavation have been properly compressed. The lower levels have been honeycombed with air pockets.

Remember the hardened clay we mentioned earlier as being the typical soil type in which water seepage problems flourish, the soil type that allows little or no water percolation except over a long period of time? Well, this dense, clay-soil combination compacts the least using today's backfilling methods. The consequence? Rainwater or spring water filters quite easily into the lower levels of the backfill area, taking advantage of the honeycomb of air pockets and clay left uncompressed by the backfilling process. The pursuant water pressure generated from sheer weight at these lower levels is massive. Before long, the pressurized water will exploit any cracks or weaknesses in the walls and seepage will occur.

THE FLOOR SLAB

But let's not get ahead of ourselves. Instead, let's examine the next stage of construction that concerns us. After the walls are built up to grade level and are resting solidly upon the footing, the basement slab will be poured into place. As shown in Figures **1** and **2**, the 4 to 6-inch thick floor is poured above the footings and is troweled into place right up against the walls. Basement floors are required by most local codes to be reinforced with wire and reinforcing bar, but I woefully report that very few of the floors I've opened up contained either. Some local codes also require a layer of plastic sheeting (polyethylene) to be stretched out around the entire basement (interior) from wall to wall on the soil before the floor slab is poured. This membrane acts as a vapor barrier" between the damp or wet soil and the floor slab (capillarity, remember?). Similarly, I must add that in the course of thousands of corrective procedures performed in basements all over the Midwest, the Northeast, the Mid-Atlantic, and the South, I found very few vapor barriers in relatively new homes. In construction, there seems to be many "slips twixt the cup and the lip." While I don't want to paint a picture of builders as being completely without scruples or incompetent, I must add that these important construction steps—so often omitted—lead to expensive repairs later in the life of the house. It took me years of observing and reasoning to uncover these basic facts and, let's face it, people are imperfect and mistakes are made in all forms of human activity. Builders are no exception to this rule. But back to our floor slab.

THE PERIPHERY FLOOR SEAM

After the floor slab is poured to a thickness of 4 to 6 inches, then troweled, and soon afterward has cured, a phenomenon takes place. When the water that acted as the catalyst for the chemical reaction taking place between the dry components of the cement (Portland cement, sand and gravel) evaporates out of the newly poured cement, the cement shrinks. A small, and in some cases imperceptible, seam will appear all around the edges of the slab where it adjoins the walls. I've seen this seam become so pronounced that one could stick a toothpick into it. This crack or opening which runs around the entire periphery of the basement is the second major entry way for water to follow as pressure builds outside the home in the backfill area. (See **Figure 1** and **Figure 2**) Most basement seepage is either through the wall or the floor seam, or through floor cracks; and some basements experience both forms of seepage simultaneously.

All basements exhibit this periphery seam, as it is an unavoidable expectation when dealing with cement. Fact: the walls of the basement *can* be made watertight with proper attention to detail and effective techniques. The floor seam, though, requires other methods, which don't repel water, but rather, control it. We are going to review a brief summary of what we've discussed so far and then we'll move on to discover how to properly water-proof a brand new home.

SUMMARY

Let's review some of the highlights of what are seen to be important facts in the story of basement construction.

- Basements often get built in soil types that don't permit quick percolation of ground-water.

- Most states require builders to warranty a basement dry for only one year pursuant to the home's construction.

- Existing construction practices do not promote or encourage careful consideration and effective techniques that are designed to ensure years of carefree basement maintenance.

- Certain problems exist due to inherent shortcomings in the materials used.

- The two major ways in which water enters the basements of our homes is through the walls and the periphery seam of the basement floor and/or floor cracks. (Window well and stairwell seepage will be covered briefly in the Chapter Four.)

- There is hope, however. There are indeed ways to make a dry basement possible, in both new construction and existing homes.

CHAPTER 2

If I Ruled the World

Certainly we all have fantasies that center around our field of expertise, whatever that may be. We conjure up images of setting wrongs to right. We do battle with mediocrity in all its malevolent forms and emerge triumphantly with everyone happily receiving their money's worth, symbolically speaking. And if wishes were horses, beggars would ride…right? Not so! I'm going to dedicate this chapter to Joe and Joanna the consumer and describe how the construction steps we've laid out so far can be accomplished differently so as to create a dry and pleasant basement needing minimal maintenance for the life of the home. Heads up, you new homebuyers!

As before, we excavate the hole for the house. We pour our footings to code and reinforce these with steel reinforcing bar. A parallel run of two #6 (3/4 inch) steel rods should be sufficient. (Some states do not require this reinforcing!) These reinforced footings will be less likely to shift and separate thus eliminating many future wall cracks. Fewer wall cracks equals less wall seepage. We are building this basement from cinder blocks. Once the walls are laid up, we apply two coats of waterproof cement parging. Each coat needs to be at least ½ to ¾ inch thick. Poured concrete walls don't require cement parging. Both types of walls, however, would then receive very careful attention when applying the waterproofing membrane.

The bituminous (tar) coating is still the most cost-effective way to begin the membrane process. However, we would not spray or brush on a paper-thin coating of liquefied tar. We would instead apply, by trowel, a fiber-reinforced thick tar. Plastic roof cement made from asphalt is ideal for this purpose. This kind of tar trowels on beautifully and it has body enough to hold on without sagging. Essentially, it behaves like cement in terms of its workability and if left alone will actually "skin over," producing a reasonably hard, non-sticky crust. But "skinning over" would not suit our purposes. No, we're going to provide a different surface for the freshly applied tar, which covers the entire wall, from the footing up to the grade level. We certainly don't want any of the asphalt coating to show above the ground level, as this would be unsightly and unnecessary.

Once the tar is applied 1/4"-1/2" thick over a section of wall, we will smooth on a sheet of thick polyethylene plastic (6 mils). These two materials complement each other very efficiently. The plastic keeps the tar green and sticky (green meaning uncured, not "skinned over") and the tar acts as a mastic, firmly bonding the plastic to the tar-covered wall. Now, when I say smooth on, I mean we'll handle the plastic panel just as we would a section of wallpaper. Starting at the footing level, the bottom of the pre-cut section of plastic will be gradually pressed into the tar all the way up to the grade level. This is a two-man job and can be done quickly with practice. Any and all big air bubbles can be pressed out in the same fashion one would employ when wallpapering the bedroom or bathroom. The panels of plastic sheeting should be 4 to 5 feet wide to ensure easy handling. This work is repeated around the entire perimeter of the structure. All overlapping joints should be at least 12 inches wide with plenty of asphalt being used under the overlap joints. I should mention, there are various rubber membranes available to accomplish the same purpose our polyethylene sheeting is serving and are used for commercial foundations deep in the ground (5-6 stories). There are also contractors who can spray on a thick rubberized coating as a membrane. The membrane is the linchpin of the wall's waterproofing system, and great care must be taken in the installation of it, regardless of the method chosen.

What we've achieved then, so far, is this: the polyethylene and asphalt membrane meld into one unit. The asphalt serves as a waterproofing barrier as well as a mastic holding the thick, water repellent, non-biodegradable plastic sheeting snug to the wall. This mutually beneficial combination of the two components, trowelable asphalt and heavy plastic becomes a long-lasting self-complementary mechanical barrier. But hold on, we're not done yet. There is more TLC to come.

BACKFILLING CORRECTLY

Before correct backfilling procedure is discussed, I will race ahead a moment and touch on a piece of a future segment's information. Some state codes require a drainage system located at the exterior footing level and running around the entire perimeter of the new basement. In order to simplify our example, I'm going to pretend that the wall we're backfilling now does not require such a system. With that out of the way, let's move on.

We've installed a beautiful watertight, consistent mechanical barrier whose effective life span is indefinite. Do you think we should expose this masterwork to the trials and tribulations of customary backfilling protocol? Not on your life! No, we're going to protect this essential yet fragile membrane against any conceivable disruption. That's why we'll now be installing a protective shield of 4 X 8-foot Styrofoam panels (rigid) around the entire perimeter of the basement walls. These panels are available at any good building supply center and are a must if dry basement walls are desired. Any quality latex adhesive can be used to adhere the Styrofoam panels to the plastic membrane. We've obtained the 1-inch thick panels since they are very effective at the job of keeping any sharp rocks, broken bottles, rusted cans and the like from inflicting any rips, tears, or miscellaneous mayhem on our recently installed membrane. The Styrofoam panels increase in cost as they increase in thickness, so the 1-inch is desirable budget-wise. Once again, every square inch of the membrane must be protected from footing to grade level by the Styrofoam panels—See **Figure 3**.

Finally, it's time to begin backfilling. Whether backfilling is done by heavy equipment or by hand, it's crucial that power tamping techniques are used to completely compact the soil going back against the walls. Gas powered tamping machines can be rented at virtually all equipment rental centers. The backfill process should go slowly and thoroughly. As each one foot layer of soil is thrown or pushed down into the excavated area, it must be thoroughly compressed. One or two men should be busy tamping and compacting all the way up to grade level. If this were done, the builder would have a lot less dirt to remove from (or spread out) around the building site. In fact, compacted soil with no trapped air pockets, particularly if it demonstrates a high clay content, is the best protection the homeowner can have against great quantities of water building up and creating pressure in the backfill area.

The soil should be gradually built up until it's slightly above (4 to 6 inches) where the final grade level will be. Even with all the laborious tamping, most soils will still settle slightly over time as rain or snow add weight and enhance compaction. We have the calming assurance provided by the protective Styrofoam panels that any settlement now occurring will not pull the plastic membrane downwards or in any other way disturb the precious watertight membrane we've provided. Also, the Styrofoam panels give excellent protection against heat loss through the basement walls in wintertime. If you think this type of attention to detail is overkill, then try doing all of this once the house is finished and landscaped. I have done so hundreds of times in order to correct a contractor's faulty initial job, usually at the expense of the homeowner. The labor cost of excavating problem walls in an existing home is expensive and subject to unpredictable weather delays. Not only do concrete patios, concrete steps, etc. need to be removed before work can begin, but they need to be replaced when work concludes. Did I mention expensive? The primary feeling the unwary homeowner experiences is frustration because the waterproofing should have been done correctly the first time. Remember the one-year dry basement guarantee? Most of these problems show up from the second year onwards. More on that later.

FOOTER DRAINAGE OR SUBFLOOR WATER PRESSURE RELIEF SYSTEMS

All right, so we've conquered the leaking wall. The methods employed will work on cinder block, poured concrete, cement block, terra cotta block, brick and stone walls—in short, all below-grade walls. These techniques are identical whether used in new construction or on a fifty-year-old home. —See Chapter 3: This Old (Leaky) House. Let's resume our story.

I'd really like to remove the shroud of mystery surrounding the subject of basement floor seepage and the steps taken to correct it. Remember, all leaking homes experience either wall or floor seepage and in some cases both varieties simultaneously. In my reign as 'king for a day" we learned how to do the proper, long-lasting job of making a wall watertight. Now I'm going to resume my kingly position and describe how I would ensure that a newly constructed home wouldn't ever have to undergo the heartbreak of basement floor seepage.

Examine **Figure 3** closely. You will observe the normal wall, footing, floor configuration that you are now familiar with. But there is one difference. Do you see the four inch perforated pipe running along the edge of the footing? This pipe is referred to in most local codes as the "common interior draintile". It is called "draintile" because in times past before the advent of petroleum-based pipes such as PVC, ADS, ABS, etc., the old types of pipes were made from terra cotta clay just like the picturesque Spanish roofing tiles we're all familiar with. The modern pipes, though, don't biodegrade, they carry water more efficiently and they are far easier to physically work with. Terra cotta clay is no longer used in the United States for pipe making, at least on a large scale, but the system you see illustrated is as old as man's ability to manufacture these terra cotta clay pipes. The system shown has been used in one form or another by all ancient civilizations from Mesopotamia to the Incas of Peru. It was used to carry water from one area to another using "gravity feed" to do the work. Concept: water flows downhill; water will not flow uphill.

FIGURE 3 PROPERLY SEALED WALL WITH SUBFLOOR RELIEF SYSTEM

PROPERLY SEALED
WALL WITH SUB-FLOOR
PRESSURE RELIEF SYSTEM

NOT TO SCALE

Usually, water transportation is thought of in terms of using solid pipes. For instance, carrying drinking water from one area to another on a downhill slope. We've all seen photographs of the ancient Roman aqueduct systems. These channels carried water from mountain springs, rivers or lakes downhill, on a gradual slope, to thirsty cities lacking sufficient water supplies of their own.

Well, what our system is going to do is the same in principle. We're harnessing the constant force of gravity and taking advantage of water's inevitable characteristic of flowing downhill. The main difference in application is the fact that we'll be using a perforated pipe, not a solid pipe. Sounds confusing? It's not!

We know that water pressure builds up beneath our basement's floor because it has nowhere else to go and therefore wants to push its way into our basement through any opening it can find. It can find ways of entry through the walls and the seam between the floor and the walls. In the case of a very old, thin, cracked floor, the water can appear in the middle floor area as well. Essentially then, the water will seek the easiest access route and pour in to relieve the pressure behind it. So, at the floor level, since we cannot seal the water out as we did with the wall, we must intercept it and control it. There is, without doubt, no way to seal the floor seam or any floor cracks against water pressure. Believe me, I've tried. Eventually the pressure will win every time. The initial tendency of most homeowners is to try to seal the periphery seam or floor cracks against the water. During the first "heavy pressure episode," the seepage ends up around legs of their favorite easy chair in the basement recreation room.

This is where the draintile comes into the picture. As stated, the pipe we are using is not solid, it is perforated. It is peppered with holes to enable water to rush into it. The high pressure situation beneath the floor will cause the water trapped under there to find the draintile and obey its own unerring property of flowing downhill. Remember that water will always seek the easiest access. It did so when it pushed its way around the footing and we are going to oblige this tendency with our 4-inch perforated pipe placed directly in its path. *Once the pressurized water enters the draintile pipe, the homeowner is in charge.* The homeowner now dictates where the water goes. As illustrated in **Figure 3**, this struggle for control all goes on beneath the floor, silently and efficiently.

The pipe, located next to the footing, encircles the entire interior of our basement. The pipe is installed so that it gently slopes, usually at the rate of ¼-inch for every 5 feet. Depending upon the depth of the footing in relation to the floor slab, the pipe can be anywhere from 8 to 18 inches deep. The sloped trench that carries the pipe runs down to a container where the water can be collected and then periodically pumped out of the house. This container is variously known as the sump well, sump crock, sump pit or sump reservoir.

This method of relieving water pressure from beneath your basement floor is absolutely the most effective, thorough and reliable in existence. There is, practically speaking, nothing else available. The trick comes with upgrading every aspect of the age-old approach so that we're truly maximizing the results hoped for.

The first upgrade is to make sure that before the concrete floor is poured, the installation of the all-important floor drainage system receives proper attention. It is essential to use only the finest materials. The pipe, for example, should be a heavy-duty crushproof 4-inch PVC. This pipe should be able to resist being crushed by the weight of the concrete workers who'll be pouring and finishing your future floor. A schedule 40 PVC 4-inch perforated pipe is adequate.

The draintile pipe should not be laid directly on the soil at the bottom of the trench, but should be elevated by 4 to 6 inches of ¾-inch gravel under the base of the pipe. This will help prevent the pipe from silting up later in its life. A gravel bed of at least 4 inches should be spread over the entire area where the floor will go. The gravel should be ¾ inch to allow quick water percolation through it. With this gravel bed in place under the entire floor, water can find its way to the draintile system from anywhere, including the middle floor. Because we're using ¾-inch gravel throughout the work, the draintile pipe should be perforated with holes no bigger than ½-inch in diameter so that no pieces of gravel can fall into the pipe.

Every aspect of the system is important. Probably the most important factor of the system's success centers on the slope of the 4-inch pipe. A level pipe will not conduct water quickly and will eventually silt up. In order to transport the groundwater quickly enough to effectively remove floor pressure, the pipe must drop, from its high point, at the rate of ¼ inch for every 5 feet of distance covered. This means in simple mathematics that the pipe will slope down an inch for every 20 feet of pipe installed. For example, the average square basement contains approximately 120 feet of perimeter. If we locate the high point of the system in the middle of the 120 feet perimeter, the pipe will drop 3 inches because the pipes will begin at the highpoint and flow downhill in both directions, hugging the footing, towards the pump container (sump well). (See **Figure 4**) On the other hand, if the draintile system was installed along a straight wall containing 120 linear feet, the high point would be located at one end of the wall. The pipe would drop 6 inches by the time it terminated into the pump container.

If at the time the home is built, it is observed that the excavated hole where the basement is to stand holds rainwater or spring water for a week or more without draining, then it would be a good idea to send a "finger" of draintile pipe through the middle floor area, in addition to the standard four-wall system. (See **Figure 4**)

Always be aware that the principal object of these sub-floor relief systems is to drain the entire floor area to a collection point as rapidly as possible. The system should be

FIGURE 4 DRAINTILE SYSTEM PLAN VIEW

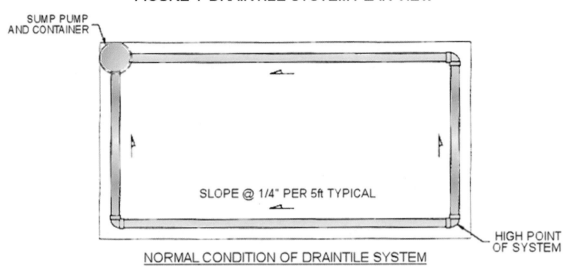

NORMAL CONDITION OF DRAINTILE SYSTEM

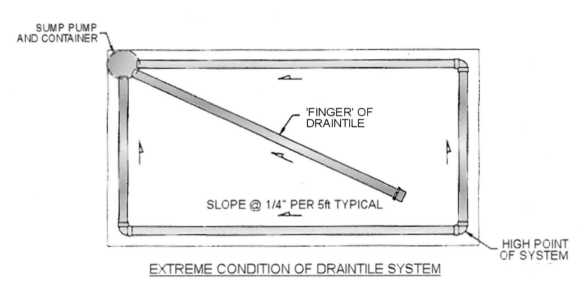

EXTREME CONDITION OF DRAINTILE SYSTEM

DRAINTILE SYSTEM PLAN VIEW

NOT TO SCALE

designed to "de-water" the sub-floor area as quickly as gravity will permit. This natural force of gravity will efficiently perform its job if you accommodate it with the attention to detail that complements and enhances its power. As you might imagine, once the basement floor is poured, it is very expensive to go back and correct oversights or shortcuts that will hamper the performance of the system.

THE SUMP PUMP AND CONTAINER

After the trenches are dug and the draintile pipe is in place and anchored down with gravel, it's time to install the electric pump setup which is the heart of the system and incidentally, the only moving part. Gravity, along with our help, has brought the water to this lowest point of the trench system and it's here that we'll dig the hole to hold the ABS plastic container which will house the electric sump pump and act as a holding reservoir for the collected water. These modern sump wells are about 2 feet in diameter, 3 feet deep and feature a tight-fitting lid.

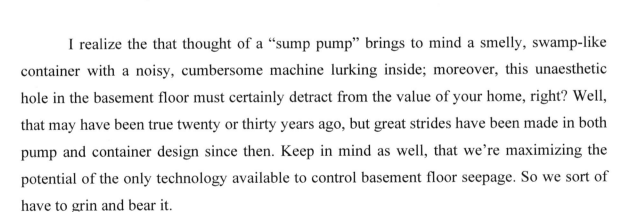

I realize the that thought of a "sump pump" brings to mind a smelly, swamp-like container with a noisy, cumbersome machine lurking inside; moreover, this unaesthetic hole in the basement floor must certainly detract from the value of your home, right? Well, that may have been true twenty or thirty years ago, but great strides have been made in both pump and container design since then. Keep in mind as well, that we're maximizing the potential of the only technology available to control basement floor seepage. So we sort of have to grin and bear it.

Hundreds of concerned housewives have expressed heartfelt reservations to me about the installation of a sump pump in their basement. But remember, many local codes now require the inclusion of a sump well and pump in new home construction, so they are here to stay.

Two factors govern the placement of the pump. Technically, it's best if the pump is placed closest to where it will be discharging its contents to the outside of the house. Pump manufacturers recommend that the number of feet of discharge pipeline be limited to reduce the resistance the water encounters as it is pushed uphill, around bends, etc. The longer the pipe, the larger the volume of water the pump has to push and the pump's ability to do so is finite. And it's equally important that this practical concern be balanced by placing the container in an unfinished area, inconspicuously, such as under the future washer or dryer.

INSTALLATION OF THE SUMP WELL AND THE PUMP

Yes, thank goodness, the new and updated containers and pumps that we make such valuable use of today are not only refined and physically quiet, but the containers are non-biodegradable and the pumps can push thousands of gallons of water over a relatively short period of time. That's right, they're pretty and they can fight! (See **Figure 5**)

As the illustration shows, the draintile pipes flow directly into the sump well. Some homes produce a great amount of water during a snowmelt or rainfall and the pipes need to vent unimpeded directly into the sump well to relieve the pressure quickly. The sump well should be surrounded by at least 6 to 8 inches of ¾-inch washed gravel. This will help prevent silting. The sump well (container) needs to be drilled on both the bottom and sides with ½ inch holes. There should be at least six holes for every square foot of surface area. As you can see by the drawing, the sump pump sits flush on the bottom of the sump well. This discharge line, usually a 1-½ inch PVC schedule 40 (solid) pipe, should exit out the side of the sump well below the floor level. This allows the concrete floor, soon to be poured, to hold the pipe firmly in place, eliminating vibration.

FIGURE 5 SUMP PUMP SETUP WITH DISCHARGE LINE

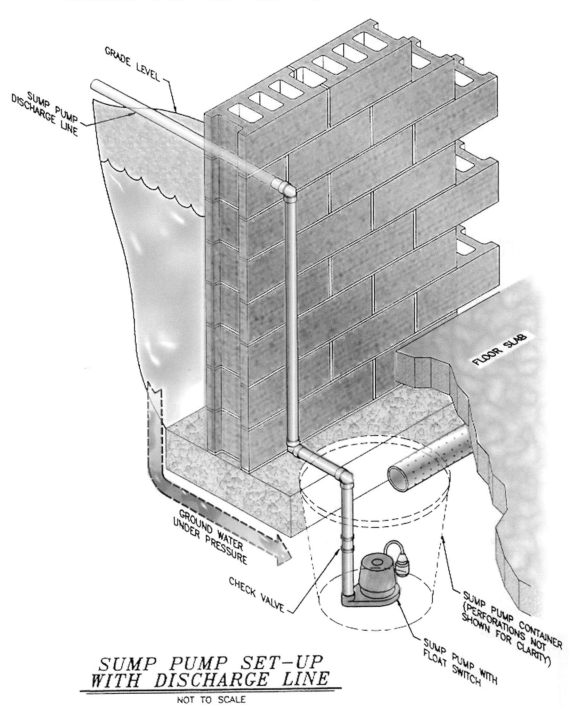

SUMP PUMP SET-UP
WITH DISCHARGE LINE

NOT TO SCALE

All sump pumps require an in-line check valve to prevent water from rushing back down into the sump well from the highest point of the discharge line once the sump pump has deactivated. I like to place the check valve directly above the pump as this minimizes the amount of water that will fall back into the sump well. The pump doesn't appreciate having to pump the same water twice and besides, not installing a check valve will void the manufacturer's warranty.

These new pumps are totally automatic. Depending upon the type, they feature either a float or a rubber diaphragm switch assembly that senses the height or weight of the water in the sump well and ejects up the discharge line at a predetermined setting. There are numerous brands of sump pumps. I like the type that are submersible and utilize an exterior float to activate the switch assembly. The switch assembly in these types of pumps is located on top of the pump, well insulated, and is rarely covered with water. The pump's "switch activation zone" is designed to keep the switch assembly high and dry most of the time. This seems, in my experience, to give the switch assembly a longer life span. I'm not going to cover in any great detail the installation of the sump pump because complete and easy to follow instructions are included with your purchase of all such pumps.

I will, though, give unsolicited praise to and recommend the 1/3-hp (horsepower) Zoeller pump. Zoeller makes a reasonably priced line of pumps ranging from 1/3 hp to 1 hp. The 1/3-hp model will handle most residential water problems. The One-horsepower model has worked in any and all situations that I have placed it, commercial or residential. (Zoeller: 1-800-928-7867.)

Over the years, I have seen sump pumps housed in the most rudimentary of containers. I've seen do-it-yourselfers use terra cotta flu liners, trashcans or just a hole in the basement floor with a pump dropped into it. Apart from the aesthetics of the pump installation, there are certain factors that will affect the performance of the sump pump. First of all, unless the pump is housed in a container which can keep gravel or small stones from coming into contact with the intake ports at the base of the pump, then the risk is always present that a piece of gravel will be drawn in and jam the impellers inside the pump. This will cause the pump to stop pumping and you've got problems.

Also, the discharge line needs to be kept stable and the new ABS containers, as seen in **Figure 5**, lend themselves well to such an installation. The line needs to go through the side of the container then, from there, up the wall and finally to the outside of the house. By running through the side, the discharge line will become very stable and the connections between the check valve and discharge line cannot vibrate loose.

Little things like the fact that your sump pump container needs to have a lid to prevent pets or small children from falling in is only common sense. The container should be large enough to house at least two pumps. The second pump, should you want one, can be installed piggyback style on top of the main pump and tied into the same discharge line. Instantly, you have the security of knowing that should the main pump fail one stormy night, the top pump will 'dewater" the basement. I have installed hundreds of backup pumps in this way for people whose homes were on active springs. Water continually runs into sump wells such as these; and should the sump pump fail, the basement would become a swimming pool overnight. Naturally, your water problem needn't be as severe as this for you to appreciate the security and peace of mind granted by the inclusion of a backup pump in your plans and budget.

If you are worried about an interruption in the electricity supplied to your home, battery backup pumps are available. These pumps aren't as rugged as the regular pumps and are intended only for short-duration emergency use. Their battery, normally a marine battery, is kept continually charged by a transformer component, which is all part of the package. To reiterate: this second pump, be it battery backup or not, can save a lot of water damage if the main pump fails. *Never, but never, let anyone tell you that your basement needs more than one sump crock.* If your basement's perimeter is 600 linear feet or more, perhaps a second container is appropriate, but the average home requires only one container into which you can put two pumps. If a house contains two sump wells because of a contractor's desire to make more money, i.e., because of greed or because a homeowner got faulty advice from a know-it-all relative, it could affect the resale value of the home. Why? Because after seeing two containers in the basement, a prospective buyer might surmise that you really have a bad water problem. Think about it! Two containers are absolutely unnecessary and a two container arrangement sends a bad signal to any potential buyers ...beware, wet basement!

THE DISCHARGE LINE

The 1 ½-inch PVC pipe that will carry the groundwater expelled from your home has to be taken as far away from the house as possible. There are some areas of the country that, under special circumstances, will allow a homeowner to vent the water into the home's main soil stack (sewer line). These special circumstances usually mean that the individual lives in a row house and the ejection of the water will create a large puddle in the neighbor's yard. Also, an active discharge line sending hundreds of gallons (these are rare) of groundwater out into a street can create a frozen lake in the winter, which can cause a real hazard to pedestrians and vehicles alike. Generally, if you find that your house is going to put out a lot of water, a permit can be obtained through the local authorities and they will allow you to run this groundwater away through the city's sanitary sewer system. This practice is frowned on, however, because if everyone who had a sump pump in their basement discharged the water in this way, the sewage treatment plants could never handle the flow.

In my experience, maybe only one house in five hundred produces this type of water flow and these homes are generally on springs. Most basements require only that the 1 ½-inch PVC discharge line be taken at least twenty feet away from the house. To prevent the line from freezing solid in the winter, the pipe must slope at least ¼ foot for every 10 feet it covers once it leaves the house. This will prevent water from standing in the line. Never take the discharge line to a so-called "dry well." The end of the line must always see daylight, and it is preferable to cover the end of the pipe with hardware cloth (wire) to stop burrowing animals from crawling into it. If you "daylight" the end of the discharge pipe, you'll always be sure that ejected water will have a wide-open pipe through which it can be easily discharged. Drywells, on the other hand, are always a mystery because you cannot observe the state of the interior because it is all below ground. It is truly tragic if your basement can tout a state-of-the-art water control system, but that system cannot function because the discharge line is terminated into a silted-up drywell that will not accept water. Similarly, it is not advisable to send the water into a septic tank, as this can adversely affect the bacterial action in the tank. Moreover, this would actually be sending the water right back into the ground, which could create a recycling syndrome whereby water pumped out of the basement soon finds its way right back *in*.

POURING THE FLOOR

Once the draintile, the pump container and pump, and the gravel bed are in place, the contractor will be ready to pour the concrete floor slab. A vapor barrier of polyethylene plastic (6 mils) should be laid over the entire 4 to 6-inch gravel bed to prevent moisture from being carried into the basement by the capillarity phenomenon. Recall the "wick action" cement displays when in contact with water. Over the plastic is laid the wire reinforcement that is standard in most state and local codes. If a strong floor is expected, this wire reinforcement must be included. Cement, regardless of how much steel reinforcement is incorporated in it, will always crack. That is its nature. This wire reinforcement will not permit these hairline cracks to expand. There is always settlement in a new home. The addition of reinforcing bar (#6) every six feet or so will help minimize the movement.

EXTERIOR FOOTING DRAINTILE

Some states currently require, as they have for many years, the inclusion of an exterior footing drainage system on all new construction (See **Figure 6**.) What is exterior footing draintile? Well, it's basically the same kind of draintile system we have used on the interior of the home. The draintile pipes encircle the exterior of the home at the footing level and are then conducted, either through the base of the wall, or under the footing (which is the preferable route) into a sump well located next to the footing in the interior of the basement. These systems have been used for forty years.

I must say, after having had the benefit of excavating hundreds of these systems, that they are more of a liability than an asset to the well being of a foundation. Originally, years ago, these systems were installed and didn't vent into the sump well inside. In fact, there may not have been a sump pump inside. Regardless, it was theorized that these systems would give the ambient water some place to go and it would then gradually dissipate into the deep subsoil. Of course, what in fact happens when you attract water to a draintile system and fail to relieve the pressure, that is, send the water to a collection point to be pumped far away, seepage occurs. Most of the time, these old exterior systems become completely silted up, the gravel and pipe having been glutted with a fine-grained mud. To correct the problems caused by the defunct system, we would excavate the wall. These old systems become like a moat around the base of the foundation. It is not unusual to see the bottom 3 or 4 feet of poured concrete become thoroughly saturated on the inside. The remedy: remove the old system, reseal the wall and if local codes require, replace the exterior draintile system with a properly installed system.

Recently, since interior draintile has been required in almost all states that are traditionally plagued with basement seepage problems, the exterior systems, if required, stand a fighting chance. At least, these exterior systems can be relieved into the sump container inside. This is an admitted improvement. But, I still don't like exterior systems.

FIGURE 6 POURED CONCRETE WALL WITH CORRECT EXTERIOR DRAINTILE SYSTEM

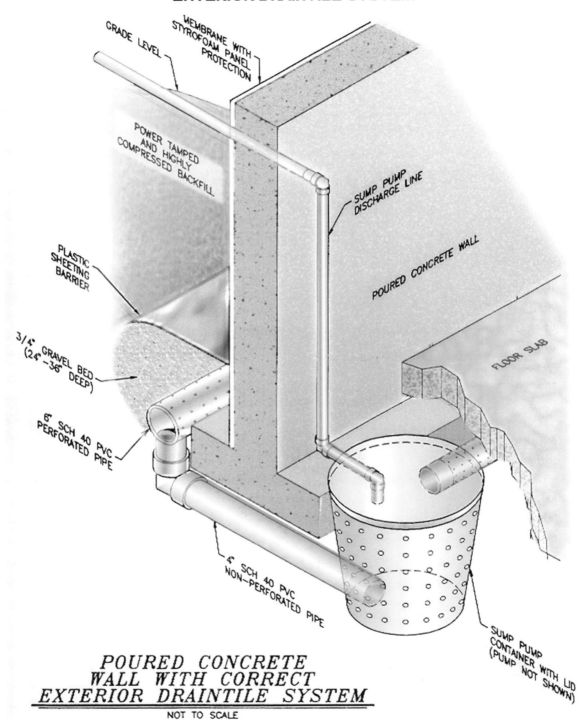

MEMBRANE WITH STYROFOAM PANEL PROTECTION

GRADE LEVEL

POWER TAMPED AND HIGHLY COMPRESSED BACKFILL

SUMP PUMP DISCHARGE LINE

POURED CONCRETE WALL

PLASTIC SHEETING BARRIER

FLOOR SLAB

3/4" GRAVEL BED (24"-36" DEEP)

6" SCH 40 PVC PERFORATED PIPE

4" SCH 40 PVC NON-PERFORATED PIPE

SUMP PUMP CONTAINER WITH LID (PUMP NOT SHOWN)

POURED CONCRETE WALL WITH CORRECT EXTERIOR DRAINTILE SYSTEM

NOT TO SCALE

Mainly, I don't approve of this practice because of the faulty way in which most home-builders tamp the backfilled soil above these exterior drainage systems. Water from down-spouts as well as ambient rainwater or snowmelt rush through this fluffed-up backfill and inundates the system below. This overwhelming infusion of water carries silt with it, and invariably the system becomes clogged up at numerous points.

The ground up at the grade level will actually settle downwards as the soil beneath it gradually feeds into the gravel and pipe below. As the ground settles, more water can collect in the resulting depression, creating even more pressure below as this water filters inexorably down. Do the words "vicious cycle" ring a bell?—See **Figure 7**.

The bottom line is this: as the exterior system, because of silting, gradually stops re-lieving pressure into the sump well inside the basement, water becomes trapped in pockets all around the outside of the foundation. Eventually, given the mediocre quality of the membranes applied to most residential structures in this country, these pockets of trapped water are going to saturate the foundation walls—it's only a matter of time.

If the local codes require that your home include such an exterior footing draintile system in the construction plans, then there are some precautions you may take to prevent silting. First and foremost, insist that a 6-inch crushproof pipe be used. Schedule 40 PVC perforated pipe will be adequate. This sized pipe is considerably larger than the 4-inch pipe usually called for. The increased size will accommodate more silt without a stoppage of water flow. Minor silting is unavoidable. There must be at least 2 feet of ¾-inch washed gravel surrounding the pipe on all sides except the base, where 6 inches of gravel is sufficient. Thick polyethylene plastic sheeting (9 mils) must cover the top and sides of the gravel and pipe system. Perforate the plastic with a few 1/8-inch holes, six per every square foot. The groundwater will find the holes easily enough. Slope the draintile pipe ¼ inch for every 5 feet of distance covered. Reduce the 6-inch pipe to 4-inch pipe before entering the inside. (See **Figure 6**)

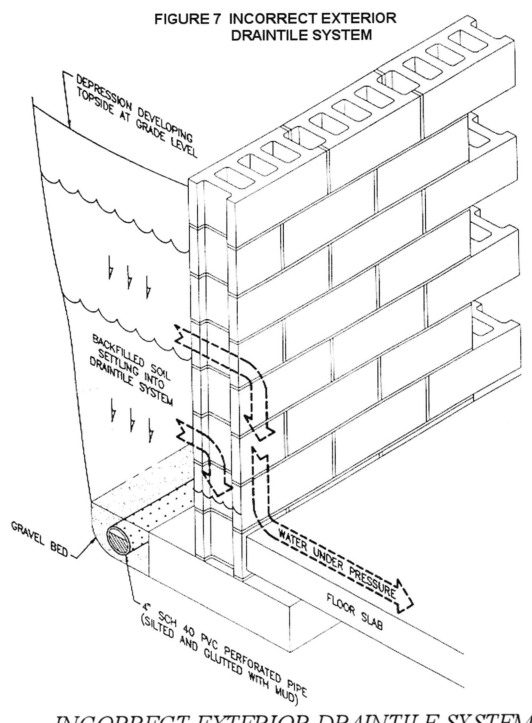

FIGURE 7 INCORRECT EXTERIOR
DRAINTILE SYSTEM

INCORRECT EXTERIOR DRAINTILE SYSTEM

NOT TO SCALE

The key to success, however, will be found in the tamping process. During backfill, every 8 to 12 inches, without fail, the soil must be power tamped all the way up to grade level. Compressing the soil in this fashion will create a natural barrier that will impede the water's flow downward toward the footing. The grade level should slope down and away from the House's walls; not dramatically, just a gentle slope is adequate. Any water that finds the exterior draintile system will be clear and silt free. Using these methods, your outside system will last indefinitely.

SUMMARY

Now, if it seems to you the reader, upon reflection, that I'm conducting a one-man campaign to discredit builders, please discount that notion. That would be judgmental and counterproductive on my part.

What I'm attempting to do is to point out deficiencies in the current methods of building and waterproofing basements and promote time-tested improvements. The buyers of these homes with water problems deserve a fair shake. In reality, what I'm trying to do is light a candle, not curse the darkness.

Keep in mind that these descriptions of how I would construct a foundation to prevent seepage problems represent real attention to detail and lots of tender loving care. They also constitute improved methodology based upon hard-earned experience. If you are building a new home, these techniques will not fail you. But what if your 5, 10, 15, 20 or 50-year-old home is undergoing water seepage problems? Then, read on because the next chapter is for you.

CHAPTER 3 ────────────

This Old (Leaky) House

So, you've purchased a 30-year-old home with a cinder block foundation. You've bought the house as is. You're certainly handy enough with carpentry and mechanical things and you feel as though you're going to save some real money and enjoy quality time spent fixing up your new, old house. The basement leaks a little, but you've got an uncle who said that some wall sealant paint is all it needs. Man, we need to talk!

If you had bought the house through conventional channels, the previous owners would have had to take care of any and all obvious and hidden problems on their own, before the sale, or risk litigation. And the buyers generally win such claims in court. The burden is on the sellers to disclose any questionable areas concerning the home's fitness for sale and habitation.

Many states require that the sellers obtain a "dry basement" certificate. This certificate is signed by a qualified professional who is certifying that the basement was dry at the time of his inspection and that the basement did not exhibit any of the telltale signs associated with long-term periodic water seepage. These certificates are generally good for ninety days. Often times, in order to procure the signed certificate, corrective work must be done by a contractor who is willing to warranty the work for at least a year. Most contractors will warranty their work for 5 years, some for longer. They will provide the customer with a service contract as part of the agreement. If the buyer wishes to obtain bank financing, these steps need to be taken. The bank doesn't want to buy a home with a questionable foundation.

Yes, the beaten path is often times the safest route—but not always. What if the contractor who corrected the basement's seepage problem, and thereby assumed the liability of guaranteeing the basement dry, goes bankrupt? A bankrupt contractor most assuredly will not honor his service contract. What if the previous owner dutifully warranties the basement for one year, and the basement leaks in the 54th week after closing? Life can be tedious at times, yes?

What I'm getting at is this: There will be situations arising around the condition of your basement that will force either you or a contractor to take remedial steps. As we've shown, service contracts might not be honored and warranties expire. This chapter is for you if you are in this position. The knowledge contained herein will enable you to make the right decisions when the time comes.

But back to the new owners of the old home who have opted, of their own free volition, to tend to their leaky basement personally. At the time Joe and Joanna bought their home, the deal seemed attractive because of the owner financing. True, they put a large sum of money down, but there were no banks involved. Hurrah! No banks! Here's how it happened.

The home is a 30-year-old rambler. It's in a nice, quiet neighborhood and the roof, brick facade and exterior paint job all look good. In fact, the interior seems very clean. The sellers, Mr. & Mrs. Smith, have done a lot of little extras to fix up the home—the freestanding wood stove, the ceiling fans, the track lighting. Joe and Joanna love it.

But when Joe opens the door leading to the basement, something is wrong. There seems to be a damp, musty smell hanging in the air, thick enough to make soup out of. As Joe slowly descends the basement steps, he feels a shaky lack of support on the last tread. He notices the base of the stringer which carries the treads is rotten, stained, and soft where it meets the floor. The basement is unfinished except for one corner where someone started to put up an inexpensive pressed-paper paneling. They installed six pieces or so before stopping their work. This paneling is delaminated at the base and is bulging slightly in the middle. In another corner, Joe finds the washer and dryer. Both are rusted around the base. The furnace also shows rust where it meets the floor, as do the metal legs of the old concrete laundry tub.

The cinder block walls received a coat of white paint ten years ago or so, according to Mr. Smith, the owner. Everywhere on the walls, there are irregular blotches of color ... black, gray, rust, purple. The walls look like a quilt and the mortar joints resemble colored stitching. The colonies of mildew are extensive. They're particularly active at the base of the wall. These living organisms, or rather, the gases they emit, are what Joe smelled at the top of the steps.

"Not to worry," says Mr. Smith. All Joe and Joanna need to do to the walls is apply a basement waterproofing paint and all will be well. A diluted bleach solution will remove the mold and mildew prior to painting. Joe agrees. After all, his Uncle Louie, the universal expert, has already endorsed these proposals. The buyers and sellers head back upstairs to begin signing the sales agreement.

Once upstairs, Joe remembers the rust on the base of the washer, the laundry tub legs, the dryer, and the furnace. And what about the rotten wood at the bottom of the stairs? Mr. Smith declares that this damage occurred when Hurricane Zelda came through back in 1979! Since then, everything has been fine to his knowledge. Of course, he doesn't go down there much what with his arthritic knees. It's a done deal. Joe and Joanna have bought their little fixer-upper dream house.

THE REALITY CHECK

The couple has been in their house for three months now. It has been a very dry summer. They've scrubbed the basement walls with stiff brushes using a half-bleach, half-water solution. They then brushed on 2 coats of a well-advertised basement masonry waterproofing paint. Joe first removed all the damaged paneling and furring strips, so the entire basement is now cheery and white.

The dry summer ends and September and October are very wet months. One and two inch rains seem to be regular occurrences on the weekends. Joe notices the mildew starting to break out again at the base of the wall. After a heavy rain, water suddenly appears at the foot of the stairs—about a gallon or so, Joe estimates. The rains continue. Soon, puddles of water are showing up by the furnace and the washer and dryer. And every wall has mildew popping out.

Finally, one particularly hard and lengthy thunderstorm leaves about an inch of water—muddy, silty water—over the entire basement floor. Joe and Joanna have signed a legally binding, uncontestable contract declaring that they have bought the house "as is." They are heartsick. Uncle Louie is mystified. But let's interrupt this unfortunate narrative and analyze what has happened thus far.

Joe purchased a basement displaying several signs, each sending a very important message. The message: this basement has leaked for years and since water problems never just go away, this basement will still leak with sufficient water pressure building up around it. Joe bought the basement during a dry spell, a mini-drought, when all that was visible were the telltale effects of previous water penetrations. Because of bad advice from an unknowing relative, the apparent honesty of the previous owners, and a gullibility based on ignorance and wishful thinking, Joe has unwittingly bought a full blown leaker. Let's briefly review those telltale signs again. When Joe entered the basement, he observed:

- The base of the steps were stained and rotted.

- Mold and mildew spreading prolifically throughout the basement.

- Paneling that had been started, but left unfinished probably because of seepage problems.

- What work has been done is rotted, delaminated and bulging. (Real wood paneling such as knotty pine is more resistant to water damage, but will show rotting and mold at its base.)

- Rust and corrosion showing where metal equipment meets the floor.

- Masonry waterproofing paint previously applied in an unsuccessful attempt to correct seepage problems.

- The owner admitting that the basement leaked, but to his knowledge, only once during an inundation caused by a hurricane.

Believe me, I've seen this familiar vignette played out hundreds of times. I've been in court over and over again to testify as an expert witness that Mr. A hoodwinked Mr. B when Mr. A knowingly sold Mr. B a leaky basement. In most cases, the trained eye can easily determine that such a basement has leaked before and, if so, for how long. This might have happened to you when you purchased your home. You might have been hoodwinked.

THE SOLUTION

Rather than leave Joe and Joanna floundering around with their seemingly insurmountable problem, we're going to introduce a note of optimism and hope into our story. Joe is going to obtain a copy of *THE COMPLETE MODERN GUIDE TO BASEMENT WATER-PROOFING*. Uncle Louie, feeling very contrite about offering up the bad advice, is going to make a present of the book to Joe. We are going to replace Joe's ignorance and frustration with accurate knowledge about his problem. We're going to arm him with tried and proven waterproofing techniques, that will enable him to truly attack and defeat his seepage problem. All's well that ends well, so let's get on with our story. We've got work to do!

CHAPTER 4

Waterproofing Your Basement on a Do-It-Yourself Basis

Since you've hopefully read the preceding pages and mentally dissected the information contained there, you are reasonably well aware of why and how your basement leaks. You've seen the way in which the author would build a basement so as to avoid potential water problems. Obviously, if you've purchased this book, your basement wasn't constructed in the recommended way; few are. But we are going to use somewhat similar techniques to correct your problem. We're going to discuss cinder block construction, poured concrete and brick construction in our do-it-yourself chapter. Even if you're already determined to have someone else do the corrective work, this chapter is valuable for you. The knowledge gained here will prove very useful later on, I can assure you. Knowledge is power, particularly when dealing with a contractor.

INSPECTING THE EXTERIOR OF YOUR HOME'S FOUNDATION

Before we can figure the scope of the procedures vital to correct your foundation's particular problem, we are going to concentrate on the exterior of the home's basement. There are some very important factors at play here that exert a direct influence on the type of seepage you're experiencing.

First, let's examine the gutter system on the house. Are all the gutters firmly attached? Are they efficiently carrying rainwater to sufficient downspouts to keep the gutter pans from overflowing onto the ground below? In any really significant "gulleywasher" of rain even properly functioning guttering will occasionally spill over with rainwater. What we're inspecting for here are gutters that are in bad repair, rusted out, sloped improperly, filled up with leaf debris and generally not doing their job. Run the garden hose into all gutter pans to make sure that the water quickly flows out of the downspout and onto the splashblock. Often times, hidden obstructions within the downspout are revealed in this way. Clear them at once. A jet stream from your hose can usually accomplish the task.

You'll remember my repeated admonitions about proper tamping and compaction of the backfilled soil around the basement walls. More than likely, if your basement is damp, mildewed or actually leaking, the backfill around your home is honeycombed with thousands of pencil-sized hollow channels leading from grade level all the way down to the footing. Your basement simply wasn't backfilled and the soil compressed with waterproofing in mind.

These channels start forming with the effects of the first rains that fall around your basement. From the day backfilling is completed, the rain and roof water find any voids and it basically "connects the dots" as hundreds of small streams surge downwards from void to void. By the time the house is a couple of years old, there exists a very efficient water drainage system created by normal rainfall around the walls of your basement. Unfortunately, the water only drains to the bottom of the original excavation hole and then stands, building pressure against the walls and floor of the foundation! Naturally then, it is desirable that you limit the amount of roofwater flowing directly into the backfill area. Do not underestimate the role that good guttering plays in the war on seepage.

Now that we've assured ourselves that the guttering system is satisfactory, let's look at where the downspouts are dumping the collected roofwater. Are the downspouts dropping the water onto a splashblock? Does the water flow briskly away from the house? Or does it disappear into a void beneath the splashblock?

It is of paramount importance that this accumulated roofwater be carried away from the house as far as possible. This can be achieved by using solid 4-inch sewer and drainpipe just below grade level, if the slope grading away from the home is sufficient. If the grade sloping away from the house is basically level, then extending the downspouts below grade is not practical. Water standing in the pipe will freeze in the winter. If this is the case, think in terms of extending the downspouts right on the surface of the ground. Using ordinary downspout stock or black ADS coil pipe (nonperforated) is acceptable and can be hidden by landscaping with vegetation and mulch. The point is, make absolutely sure that the water discharged from the downspout is taken as far away from the backfill area as possible, as aesthetically as possible. Eight to ten feet away should be adequate in most cases. Even if the house has been properly backfilled, this objective is still prudent.

INSPECTING FOR VOIDS AND LOW AREAS AROUND THE FOUNDATION

Most homes over two years old (depending upon the frequency of rainfall) will show obvious signs of backfill settlement, which anyone can identify. If there is a concrete patio or a stair stoop adjoining the home, there are voids forming under them. Voids are extremely common under splashblocks. The genesis of a void is very rapid under the right conditions. As rainwater, snowmelt or roofwater flow under a concrete patio, for example, that has been placed over the backfill area, the water causes the soil beneath the slab to compact very slightly. As the weight of the water causes the soil to compact, a small hollow or gap forms between the soil and the patio slab. During the next rainfall, water will hit the patio and flow to the edges. The water will adhere, through the action of its surface tension, to the sides of the slab and flow down, wrap around, and actually cling to the underside of the slab. The water will then travel a small distance and finally drop off into the small hollow formed by previous rainfalls. Consequently, the gap slowly grows bigger and bigger and can hold more and more water. The increased amount of water means more weight and soon enough a self-perpetuating void is created—all thanks to incorrect backfilling. Remember that the catalyst is the water. The more ambient water that finds the void, the bigger the void becomes. The bigger it becomes, the bigger it can become. Get the picture?

On the older homes, say 25 years and older, patio slabs can sink so much that they crack and actually slope towards the basement wall. When this happens, it's best to remove the slab, fill the void with power-tamped clay, and replace the concrete. You might imagine how much water is concentrated and channeled directly down to the home's footing under such conditions. A broken and wrongly sloped slab can direct thousands of gallons of water to just where you don't need it—See **Figure 8**.

People ask me, "Where did all the soil that was once under the slab, stoop, splashblock, etc. disappear to?" Good question! Well, a lot of the area that sank was filled with air pockets because of faulty backfilling practices. Once the soil, even hardpan clay, becomes saturated with water and liquefied, it flows in all directions. It will migrate into exterior draintile systems below it, into adjacent air pockets, and in many cases, into wall cracks, and from there into the basement itself. I've observed once hollow cinder block walls become completely filled with clay soil, washed in by water flowing from an exterior void. If silt washes directly into your basement, it's almost a foregone conclusion that a void and an accommodating wall crack are to blame.

If a concrete stoop is tilted or has sunk a few inches below its original position, there is a void beneath it, preceding its slow descent. Should a covered concrete porch, placed over the backfill area sound hollow when you walk or jump on it, it is voided underneath. To thoroughly rectify the seepage problem, these voids must be exposed and filled with power-tamped clay. If such action is simply too expensive, then power tamping the soil around these concrete structures can be helpful if they haven't settled too much. This will, at least, collapse the channels leading to the voids. One way or the other, for the welfare of your foundation, we need to impede the rapid flow of water into the voids, if we cannot eliminate the voids themselves. In tandem with all we have so far discussed, I will mention that all surface depressions or low spots need to be power tamped to collapse any channels hidden there and then brought up to grade level with power tamped clay.

FIGURE 8   SEQUENCE OF VOID FORMATION AND COLLAPSE

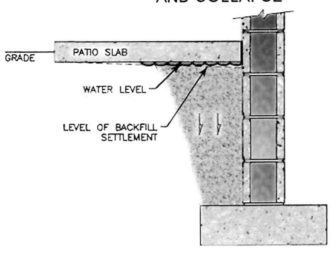

BEGINNING OF VOID FORMATION

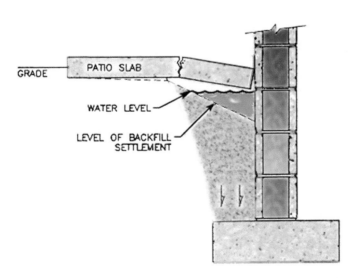

FINAL COLLAPSE OF SLAB

SEQUENCE OF VOID FORMATION AND COLLAPSE

Not to Scale

FOUNDATION WALLS
CINDER BLOCK

As we've noted, cinder block walls are hollow. Poured concrete walls, as well as brick and stone walls, are solid. Because of the obvious difference seen between Figures **1** and **2**, the methods used to treat hollow versus solid walls can be quite different. We're going to discuss cinder block walls first, since they are, nationally speaking, the most numerous.

First, allow me to make a sweeping statement. All types of below-grade walls, because they are cementitious, will inevitably develop cracking over time. You see, cement has no elasticity. For example, if the slightest movement occurs in a mortar joint, a crack will form. Cement cannot stretch, so it moves by cracking.

But back to my sweeping statement. Since all below grade walls (although I once saw a treated wood below-grade wall in a great deal of trouble) incorporate cement in their construction, we can logically deduce that all below-grade walls develop cracking, ranging from hairline size to large rips ½ to ¾ inch wide. There are many reasons why this cracking occurs. If the original construction was top notch, then the cracking below grade is minimal, limited to the hairline variety. Sometimes this is because ample steel reinforcement was included during construction. On the other hand, if shortcuts were taken in the interests of saving time and money, this cracking can be severe.

Here's an example: If the home's footing is not poured thickly enough or wide enough to carry a home's weight (30 to 50 tons and more), settling subsequently occurs. Settlement means movement and movement means cracking. I hope you remember that the leak-proof house I constructed in Chapter Two started with a footing that was not only wide and deep enough, but was also reinforced with #6 (3/4-inch) steel rods. Negligible footing movement can be achieved with careful attention to detail and with educated hands controlling the purse strings. Don't save a penny now, only to spend a dime later.

Cracking can also occur if a wall isn't allowed enough time to cure to full strength before backfilling begins. I have seen green, uncured walls being backfilled because of some deadline or another. The weight of the soil going back presses against the wall and breaks the weak, uncured bond between the blocks. Once the bond between cinder blocks and mortar joints is broken, they cannot "knit" back together again. They've lost their structural integrity forever. In other words, a cinder block wall that has been backfilled too soon after construction can be transformed from a solid, integrated unit into a series of disconnected sections being held together only by the weight of the wall above. Held together, that is, until water builds up in the backfill area during heavy rains or snowmelt and exerts pressure on the wall. The weakened wall will move and the hairline cracks born during backfilling will begin to stretch. This allows water and silt to enter. Be assured that a hopelessly thin coat of liquefied asphalt will not bridge the gaps. And if there is plastic sheeting, the water would have gotten around it with ease, as it is not bonded to the wall. And out comes the Wet-Vac…

So these are some of the reasons why cementitious walls develop cracking. Notice in **Figure 1**, the cinder block wall, in most instances, doesn't permit the water penetrating its outer shell to run directly through and into the basement. Ninety-five percent of the time the water pushing through the outer shell will run down the interior of the wall's hollow cavities and build up in the base of the block's interior. You'll observe that I have included an arrow depicting water flowing straight through the wall. This happens if a cinder block is filled with concrete. This will obstruct the downward flow. Let me explain. As a mason builds a cinder block wall, the excess wet mortar scraped from the outside mortar joints many times is thrown into the hollow wall and discarded. Sometimes enough mortar builds up to form a solid cavity filled with concrete that has been caught there. Should an exterior crack be coincidentally located just above this solid cavity, then the water flowing into the wall simply runs across the solid cavity and into the basement. This kind of situation needs to be corrected from the outside by sealing that area as described in Chapter Two. (See **Figure 3**)

This calls for an excavation to get to the problem area. *Don't be fooled by anyone telling you they can solve severe wall seepage from the inside.* If you try to get something for nothing, you'll get nothing for something. Excavation can be expensive and difficult, but you'll only cry once. Attempting to solve severe wall seepage from the inside will only lead to many frustrating and piecemeal attempts with little chance of lasting success. Mind you, once the wall is excavated, it is crucial that it is sealed properly, (see Paragraphs 3 through 12 of Chapter 2) or you'll be digging it up again.

Because wall cracks are responsible for virtually all wall seepage, it is smart to thoroughly inspect the entire exterior of the foundation for any signs of visible wall cracks. If you see a vertical wall crack, it's probably the result of a broken footing. The wall on either side of the break settles independently under its own weight and a large, vertical crack develops from the footing to the top of the wall. Paneling or Sheetrock may cover these cracks on the inside, but they are always visible on the outside. (See my publication, <u>Using Modern Structural Reinforcement Techniques to Stabilize Below-Grade Wall Movement.</u>) Be prepared to excavate and seal any such wall cracks.

SUMMARY

To summarize, we have concluded the following.

- Water penetrating through the outside shell, following hairline or larger cracks, usually flows down into the bottom course of blocks in a cinder block wall.

- Sometimes water will flow straight through a cinder block wall because of a solid cavity. This requires excavation.

- Large, visible cracks need to be sealed from the outside. This means an excavation.

- If a cinder block wall shows a great deal of the last two problems mentioned above, then it must be excavated in its entirety. That's right, the whole wall needs to be dug up and exposed all the way down to the footing. This will enable the homeowner or contractor to reseal the wall as outlined in Chapter Two, Paragraphs 3-12.

IMPORTANT BULLETIN

Now hear this! Most waterproofing contractors really dislike exterior excavations. Keep that fact in mind. We'll come back to that later.

TREATING NORMAL CINDER BLOCK SEEPAGE

When I refer to "normal" cinder block seepage, I mean seepage that is coming through the exterior wall shell, and flowing down within the hollow wall and finally pooling in the bottom course of the cinder block wall. (See **Figure 1**) Most often, this water will collect in the cavities and proceed to slowly bleed through the inside shell of the block and onto the basement floor. Although this kind of seepage appears to be very severe, it's actually the least expensive to solve. Why? Because it can be corrected by using the most basic of all waterproofing systems. The sub-floor pressure relief system is the fundamental building block used most often in taking care of general water problems. The sub-floor system always controls floor seepage problems, as we've discussed previously. And it's perfect for assisting in draining cinder blocks holding trapped water. It is tried and proven and extremely cost effective.

THE SUB-FLOOR PRESSURE RELIEF SYSTEM

Please look back to **Figure 5**. You will see the wall, floor and footing configuration that we've talked about so much. You see the draintile and sump pump setup. This system is a time-tested basic and I employ it because, first of all, it controls floor pressure. Regardless of how well we fill and power tamp the backfill voids, or how studiously we maintain our guttering, or how perfect the grading around our home, rainwater and snowmelt will still seep into the soil directly surrounding our basement. We cannot prevent that from happening. As we've seen, this water will ultimately put pressure on the floor of our basement. (Of course, some homes are on active springs and cannot do without a sub-floor draintile system.)

And yes, this publication is entitled *The Complete Modern Guide to Basement Waterproofing*, and I am advocating the use of a system as old as mankind's sense of engineering. Why? Because function is beauty ... it works. Beyond that, as well as picking up, reducing and controlling floor pressure, it helps lessen, to a limited degree, the pressure on the walls. As the draintile and pump duo control and eject the floor water, the water standing around the walls can gradually feed downwards. This is a very slow and subtle process, but the longer the system is in, the more channels the water will create to enhance this downward movement.

In a narrow way, the system can very specifically benefit the "normal" cinder block wall seepage. Here's how: Because the draintile system is hugging the footing all the way around the perimeter and running right under the course of blocks holding trapped water, we can create a happy marriage just by drilling ¾-inch relief or "bleeder" holes in each cavity of each block. The water will obey gravity and flow out of the block and into the "arms" of the system waiting below. Presto! No more trapped water in the blocks—See **Figure 9**.

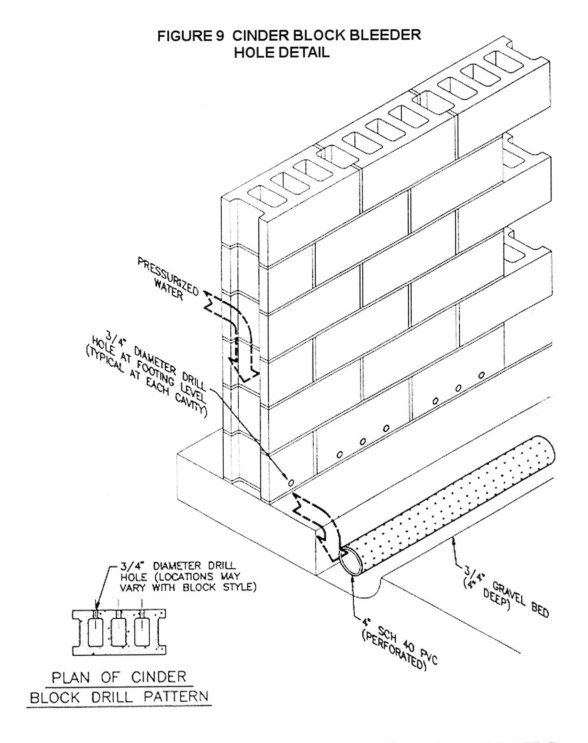

FIGURE 9 CINDER BLOCK BLEEDER
HOLE DETAIL

PRESSURIZED WATER

3/4" DIAMETER DRILL
HOLE AT FOOTING LEVEL
(TYPICAL AT EACH CAVITY)

3/4" DIAMETER DRILL
HOLE (LOCATIONS MAY
VARY WITH BLOCK STYLE)

PLAN OF CINDER
BLOCK DRILL PATTERN

3/4" GRAVEL BED
(4" DEEP)

4" SCH 40 PVC
(PERFORATED)

CINDER BLOCK BLEEDER HOLE DETAILS

NOT TO SCALE

There are other benefits derived from releasing this pooling water from the cinder blocks. The rainwater falling from our skies these days has a lower pH reading than ever before. Some American cities regularly receive rainfall registering as low as 4.5 to 5.5 on the pH scale. That reading approximately matches the acidity of tomato juice. When this acid rainwater percolates down through the highly acid clay soils, which are characteristic of many areas with seepage problems, its pH drops even further. The offshoot is that this water can, over time, induce a dissolving effect on cinder block, causing it to weaken structurally.

You see, cinder block is made from Portland lime, stone cinder, and sand. The extruded blocks are steamed at a high temperature until they are hard. The lime (cement) is the "glue" of the cinder block, holding the other components together. The acid water reacts with the alkaline lime and causes it to "effloresce." The soluble salts leach out of the block and return to their crystalline form. All cementitious walls, even brick, will fall prey to this phenomenon. We'll come back to efflorescence and it's relation to masonry waterproofing paints, but for now, be aware that the acid water can gradually diminish the strength of a block wall by pooling inside the bottom course.

This constant contact can have dire consequences as it inevitably promotes disintegration of the block. If you see your basement walls displaying a curious white powder, you're seeing efflorescence. The peculiar wick action called capillarity, which cementitious walls all have in common, will frequently draw water higher from saturated lower courses of block into blocks standing above them. These blocks can also show efflorescence and will "kick" off any kind of paint as the lime crystals "flower" out. I've seen blocks so badly weakened by acid water that I could poke my index finger through the inside shell with very little effort. Such a compromised condition won't permit a cinder block to do a very satisfactory job of holding up a house, I can tell you. Efflorescence will negate masonry paints.

OK, so we've limited the water gaining access to the backfill area, we've relieved and controlled the floor pressure, and we've released the "acid water" from the cinder blocks' lowest cavities now what? Well, we re once again going to exploit the hollow wall and introduce some airflow into the structure. This airflow will dry out the inside face of the wall and help to keep the entire interior of the wall fresh and dry. Please look at **Figure 10**. This plate, the "wall vent plate" is made from 22 gauge steel which has been galvanized. In form, it resembles a piece of aluminum siding, but it has more rigidity and differs slightly in design because of the job it performs. Now look at **Figure 11**, which shows how we are going to use this plate. The wall vent plate will be used to cover an additional set of air holes, placed above the original bleeder holes which were drilled to release water. Now look at **Figure 12** to observe the side view of the wall vent plate in juxtaposition to the floor slab. Note the arrows showing the airflow into the wall.

This air induction design is extremely effective. However, it must be noted, that its strengths can only apply to "normal" cinder block seepage. It cannot and will not supplant the virtues of excavation and the resealing of a wall from the exterior. It will not rescue a wall that is permitting copious amounts of water to enter through the outside shell. If a wall is excavated from the outside and resealed in its entirety, the wall vent system isn't needed. Don't be tricked by anyone claiming that such a system can cure an extremely degraded cinder block wall. I've seen people pay a lot of money for such a system, or a modified version, when in reality what they needed was an excavation. Remember that only walls with water in the bottom course of blocks will respond to draining and air induction. Walls that are habitually soaked or show water coming right through require excavation and resealing. Don't pay for something that won't solve your problem!

When using the wall vent system, most of the drying goes on in the wintertime. The hollow interior of the wall is very cold and will tend to draw the warm, dehumidified air from the basement in through the air holes covered by the vent plate. The vent plate

FIGURE 10 WALL VENT PLATE DETAIL

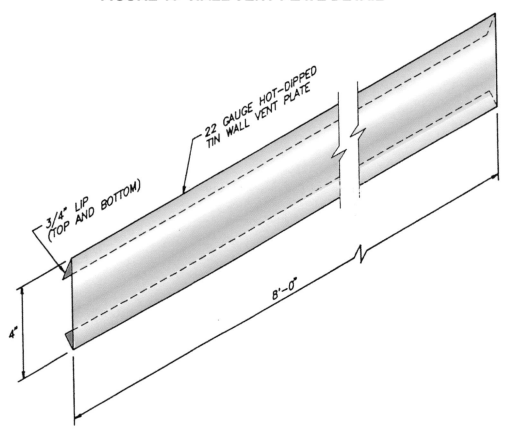

WALL VENT PLATE DETAIL
NOT TO SCALE

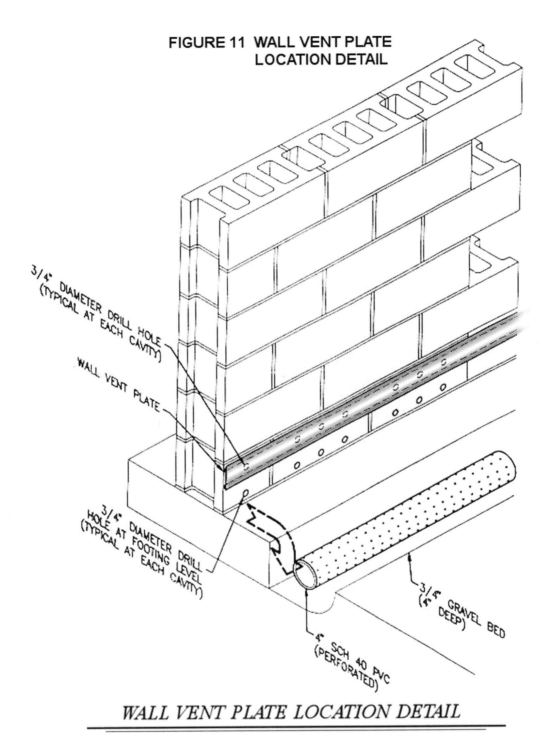

FIGURE 11 WALL VENT PLATE
LOCATION DETAIL

3/4" DIAMETER DRILL HOLE
(TYPICAL AT EACH CAVITY)

WALL VENT PLATE

3/4" DIAMETER DRILL
HOLE AT FOOTING LEVEL
(TYPICAL AT EACH CAVITY)

4" SCH 40 PVC
(PERFORATED)

3/4" GRAVEL BED
(4" DEEP)

WALL VENT PLATE LOCATION DETAIL

NOT TO SCALE

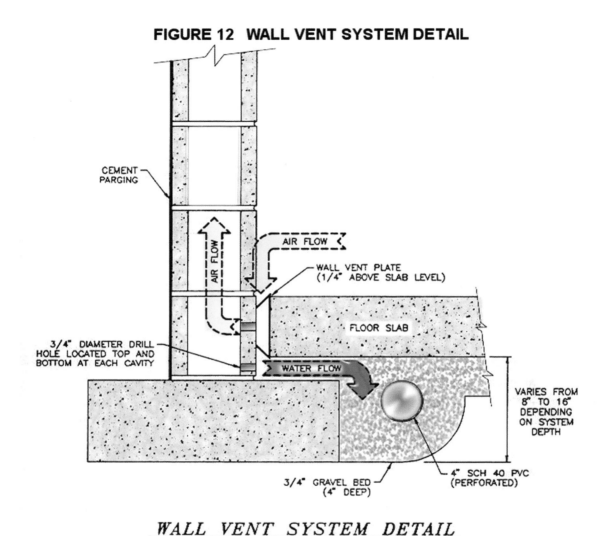

FIGURE 12 WALL VENT SYSTEM DETAIL

WALL VENT SYSTEM DETAIL
NOT TO SCALE

provides the narrow gap through which the valuable airflow passes between the floor and the wall. There is no real significant heat loss to speak of, but what little heat is pulled into the wall will intensify the drying out operation and hence is desirable. Once the inside face of the cinder block wall has dried out, the air induction will keep it dry.

We've discussed the sub-floor system and cinder block walls and the relationship between them. I am aware that so far in this overview I have not really told you how to personally accomplish any of the methods described, but be patient. For now, I'd like to continue on with a consideration of each of the two solid wall types, poured concrete and brick.

POURED CONCRETE

Poured concrete walls have been around since Roman times. In Rome, the famous antiquity, the Coliseum, is constructed largely from poured concrete. So obviously, this material is strong and long lasting and can make a very fine basement. It has a limitation, though, and that is its tendency towards cracking. These cracks, found in all concrete structures, will allow water to pass through, offering little or no resistance.

Please go back to the depiction of a poured concrete wall in **Figure 2**. It's immediately discernable that there are no hollow cavities, as with the cinder block wall. Therefore, the seepage will flow either through the periphery floor seam, or directly through the wall cracks. Simple, yes? Having made this observation, we can safely conclude that the sub-floor pressure relief system is a specific, as always, for controlling water pushing through the floor seam or any miscellaneous floor cracks. One problem down, one to go.

The wall problems revolve around the routinely found cracking that is typical of all poured concrete structures. I've seen poured concrete walls only 6 months old undergoing severe water penetration because the cracking was so severe. Insufficient steel reinforcement and/or too short a curing time and too much pressure on "green" cement during backfilling are two common problems. Substandard footings, which allow for too great an overall settlement, is a third.

There is another condition that comes into play all too often. A large foundation may need 3 or 4-cement truck's worth of concrete to complete the job. If there is an unavoidable delay between trucks so that the earliest load has time to "skin over," the next batch won't knit with the now hardened batch. There will always be a seam there. The primary shortcoming though, as far as seepage is concerned, rests with the membrane. A poured concrete wall will normally contain enough reinforcement to restrict its movement to a minimum, but the membrane ... now that's another story. You all know by now how the membranes are handled on new construction and therein lies the problem. The most minute hairline crack will allow water penetration if the waterproofing membrane is faulty and the water pressure great enough.

Now, many so-called experts will tell you that these areas where water has penetrated a poured concrete wall can be corrected by applying a sealant, be it cementitious or rubberized in nature, to the surface. They claim that if you chip out, and V-groove the crack or hole, you can get a good "grab" on the wall and anchor a mechanical barrier on that section. I cannot be emphatic enough on this point. I've seen this approach work maybe 5% of the time, on only the tiniest of pinholes. And I'm being generous with the 5% figure. There are many kinds of products available . hydraulic cement that expands as it sets, polyethylene caulking that lasts indefinitely, sealants that are brushed on, etc. The products are all fine. But, if you put them on the inside of the wall, you're putting them on the wrong side. Eventually, they won't hold, or the wall won't hold them. The wall is always moving, imperceptibly, but moving nonetheless. Over time, the barriers, if placed on the inside, will work loose. The pressure of the water will inevitably win out, as it works in concert with the movement of the wall. Don't forget, these cracks formed originally because of movement. The interior seals will, sooner or later, become dislodged and hence ineffective. Seepage will occur.

If, however, you excavate the wall to the extent that the problem area demands, then reseal that area using the methods put forth in Paragraphs 3 through 12 of Chapter 2, your work will last for the life of the home—guaranteed. This assurance is particularly valuable if you intend to cover these leaking areas with paneling and cover the floor beneath them with carpet. The universal problem is that too many people have time to do a repair two or three times incorrectly, but can't find time to do it once correctly. It is true, excavating is more initial work, but it lasts forever, if properly done. No second-guessing, no second thoughts, no Wet-Vacs, no damaged belongings.

But, you may ask, "What if the area that is leaking is not accessible from the outside, making it infeasible to excavate and reseal it?" There may be a room addition, an elaborate patio or a raised porch with steps. Here's the only recommendation I can make. If the area that is leaking is a crack, clean the wall with a wire brush. Get all loose particles off the wall. Torch the area until it's dry. Cover the crack ½-inch thick with a product called NP1. This is made by Sonneborn Building Products of 7711 Computer Avenue, Minneapolis, Minnesota 55435 (telephone 612-835-3434). This is a one part polyurethane sealant. I am making an unsolicited recommendation of this product because I have had good results with it. Install a sub-floor system on the wall where the crack is located. Do not cement it up. Allow the first layer of Sonalastic NP1 to setup overnight and go over it again, overlapping the edges. This sealant will stretch as the wall flexes. Use a piece of rigid Mylar plastic to cover the entire area to a distance of two feet on either side of the crack. This type of plastic is available in 4' by 8' sheets. The plastic can be attached to the wall with nylon nail drives. The plastic should be long enough to extend below floor level and into the gravel bed of the sub-floor system. Seal the edges of the plastic to the wall with NP1. When the floor is cemented back (this process is explained later in the book), you've created a closed channel that will direct any water compromising your seal right down into the draintile system. This is an extreme measure to take, but necessary only if you cannot gain access to the problem area from the outside. Ordinarily there would be no reason to install a sub-floor system to correct a leaking wall crack in a poured concrete wall. You would simply excavate the crack and reseal the wall from the outside. As you can see, I have no faith whatsoever in any technique which advocates sealing a wall from the inside ... and I've seen and tried them all. That's the power of experience. We want repairs that will last for the long run.

BRICK WALLS

I have not included an illustration of a brick wall because, for our purposes, a brick foundation wall can be treated exactly as we would correct a poured concrete wall. Brick walls are generally much older than their poured concrete counterparts. Their use was most prevalent before World War II and stretching all the way back to colonial times. Many of the restored townhomes found in trendy locations around our modern cities are older homes built on brick foundations.

Brick walls, it is worth noting, virtually never have concrete footings like modern walls. Rather, they have a brick footing that flares out and then narrows where the main body of the wall will be—the wall and the footing are one integrated unit. Most of the floors that are found in such homes are very thin, about 2 inches thick, having been poured long before there were local building codes. This can be a liability.

Once again, if such a home shows seepage where the floor meets the wall, classic periphery seam seepage, then the standard sub-floor pressure relief system is in order. These old, thin floors routinely show severe cracking, with moisture poking through everywhere. A four-wall system should correct this condition. If the floor is extremely thin, a new reinforced floor might be necessary in addition to the draintile system. NP1, the polyurethane product that I previously recommended, does an excellent job of sealing floor cracks, once the pressure has been removed by the sub-floor system.

What about brick wall seepage? Who can guess what I insist upon to preserve, protect and make watertight this old brick wall? You've got it, if you guessed *reseal the outside* of the wall. A brick wall has thousands of mortar joints. These are places where two different materials are joined together, fired clay bricks and sandmix mortar. If you've ever cleaned mortar off of bricks, you'll know that the bond between the two is tenuous at best. There is always a microscopic gap between them, too small for the human eye to see, but large enough for pressurized water to squeeze between. A brick wall that is 50 years old or more provides thousands of points for water infiltration if the original external waterproofing membrane is compromised. And the odds of survival for the original membrane are slim, if not nonexistent. If there is enough water pressure in the surrounding ground, such a wall will leak profusely.

I've done a good deal of work in the Georgetown area of Washington, D.C. Anyone familiar with this section of the nation's capitol knows that it is comprised of hundreds of old brick homes worth a lot of money because of proximity to the downtown Washington, D.C. business corridor. Some of these homes are over 200 years old. The below grade mortar joints are many times nothing but sand. The cement (Portland lime) component has long since leached out of the walls because of seepage. It was in this "laboratory" that I realized that stopping the water on the outside of the wall is essential if a wall, any type of wall, is to be kept dry, let alone kept intact and standing.

Having said that, I will offer this: If for one reason or another you absolutely cannot excavate a wall, maybe because of obstructions or the lack of space due to a closely neighboring home, there is an alternative way to make a basement usable. However, this should only be done after you have exhausted all possibilities of an excavation.

I previously mentioned using 4' X 8' sheets of thin, rigid Mylar plastic to form an interior shield and vapor barrier in conjunction with a sub-floor pressure relief system. These sheets cannot preserve or protect the wall, but they can make the space feel dry and you'll never see any water. Your problem may be minor and the walls won't suffer any real biodegradation. On the other hand, the seepage through the walls might be severe and yet, the walls still might maintain their structural integrity for decades. This is a judgment call for you, the homeowner or a structural engineer to make locally. I can only provide a general expectation based on past experience. There are many variables, but remember, there is no real substitute for excavation. However, the Mylar sheets can be attached to the brick wall with nylon nail drives (1/4 inch X 1 inch). These nails are thin aluminum shanks surrounded by a plastic jacket. You drill a ¼ inch hole, 1 inch deep, through the sheet and into the wall. A fastener is inserted, the nail is struck with a hammer and as the nail goes in, the plastic jacket expands. Six fasteners per sheet will very satisfactorily anchor the sheet to the wall. You will cover the entire problem area with overlapped sheets from grade level to below floor level and into the draintile system. This is a two-person job for sure. The sheets should overlap by about 2 inches. A bead of NP1 sealant can be applied between sheets to provide an absolute vapor barrier. With the sheets in place, any water coming through the wall will flow behind the plastic sheets and down into the draintile system. The sheets should project down deeply into the gravel bed (see **Figure 12**, Wall Vent Side View) so that no cement from the floor could hinder the water flow.

Since we've talked so much about installing a sub-floor pressure relief system in an existing home, let's go into detail.

INSTALLING THE SUB-FLOOR PRESSURE RELIEF SYSTEM IN AN EXISTING HOME

Even if you, the reader, don't actually install a sub-floor system, this upcoming description will certainly help you to evaluate the job done by any contractor you may hire. Knowledge is power when insisting on the best job you can obtain.

If you're thinking that it certainly would have been much easier to install a sub-floor system before the hard, thick concrete floor was in place, you're precisely right! Don't be dismayed though. Every day hundreds of contractors nationwide are installing systems like this with minimal headaches and as is often the case, the concerned homeowner with a do-it-yourself "bent" will take more care and do a cleaner job than his professional counterparts.

Now that we've had our pep talk, let the work begin.

Our first concern is to determine where we're going to put the system—along which walls. Generally, I like to do all four walls of a basement at once. In other words, even if only one or two walls, or the floor in front of them shows seepage, I prefer to treat the entire basement. My reasoning? Well, the walls have all been in the ground the same number of years. The same minimal waterproofing techniques were employed on each wall. The same type of non-draining clay surrounds the house. And a house ages and deteriorates, at least the parts exposed to the elements, just like a person does. Each day that goes by, a home's foundation develops more cracking and its original wall protection diminishes in value.

Without doubt, the final decision about the scope of the work to be done is yours. Should your resources be limited or if you're absolutely certain that by doing one or two walls you'll be taking care of your problem then, so be it. In the case of a person living in a row house or a townhouse and only the front or back wall leaks, then the decision is an easy one. In the end, you can always add on to a system if further problem areas develop.

Before starting work, you must obtain a permit if so required. Many states and counties therein do not require permits, many do. If they do, you'll need two copies of a simple schematic showing the type of system you intend to install. You have permission to use my depiction of the system in **Figure 5** for this purpose. You can expect a visit from a county and possibly a city inspector during the work. If you hire someone before the work starts, always insist to see the contractor's permit. The permit should be posted in a conspicuous place.

Once you've determined the scope of the work to be done, and obtained any permits required, you'll need to locate all underground wiring, the cold water line, the sewer line, and any other pipes, conduits, etc. that may be under the floor slab. You do this by searching for any pipes that clearly disappear into the slab. As you break the floor, stay at least 6 to 8 inches away from these pipes. This area can be tunneled later. Believe me, the business end of an electric demolition hammer doesn't have any nerve endings. It will sever a copper cold water line (main water line) in a fraction of a second. It will shatter a cast iron sewer pipe effortlessly. So be careful and go slow. Once you've located these obstructions, you're ready for a visit to your local rental center.

You can rent an upright electric demolition hammer at any good, well-stocked rental center for around $60.00 a day. You'll need a 3-inch chisel bit and a pointed bit. Rent also a rotary hammer capable of handling a ¾-inch drill bit as well as a 1½-inch diameter bit. The rotary hammer will run about $40.00 a day. You'll need a pick, a flat shovel, a round point shovel, a small mortar pan, a cement mixing hoe, a cement finishing trowel (12 inch), bolt cutters and a hacksaw. These tools will get you going; they are the basics.

Here are the steps you'll take to get the job done. Never use an air hammer; these throw too much dust.

- Grab the big demolition hammer. Using the pointed bit, break the floor directly next to the wall. Keeping your feet away from the bit, for safety reasons, break the floor directly next to the wall. (First, though, remove any floor tiles as they may contain asbestos.)

- Using the pick, dig the concrete out and find the footing. It will be located anywhere from directly under the slab to 18 inches down. Cut any wire or reinforcing bar with the bolt cutters.

- Determine how wide the footing is by cutting the floor towards the middle of the room. Once you've found the edge of the footing, you'll need to cut a further 8 inches into the middle floor area. This will make for a trench large enough to comfortably allow room for the 4-inch ADS perforated coil pipe and 2 inches of ¾-inch washed gravel on either side. The ADS is standard for this type of job.

- You have now established the width of the trench. This trench will run parallel to the wall on all problem areas. Use the 3-inch chisel bit once you get rolling.

- The depth of the trench should start at 12 inches. This should give space for 4 inches of gravel under the pipe, 4 inches for the ADS pipe, 2 inches of washed gravel on top of the pipe and 2 inches of concrete for the floor surface. Drop the grade ¼ inch for every 5 feet.

- As you dig the trench along the wall, keep the footing clean of all debris—clay, broken cement, etc.

- Be careful of pipes. Stay 6 to 8 inches away from all pipes. Break the floor on either side and continue on.

- Tunnel under the section of unbroken, intact floor by hand using a small pointed trowel. This will protect all pipes, copper or cast iron, from being broken, cracked, or otherwise harmed.

- Tunnel under the hot water heater, furnace, or any other obstruction that would be too expensive to move and replace. If the wall leaks heavily behind such obstructions, it will need to be excavated from the outside and resealed.

- Locate and dig the hole for the sump well. Dig the hole large enough for 4 to 6 inches of ¾-inch washed gravel to be placed around the perforated container. The container should be drilled with a ½-inch bit at least six times per each square foot area.

- Fit the sump well into the excavated hole and anchor the base in with about one foot of gravel.

- Using a 4-inch hole saw, drill the hole(s) for the ADS coil pipe to enter the crock. The pipe should extend 1 to 2 inches into the sump well.

- Drill a hole 1 ½ inches in diameter near the top of the well to allow the discharge line (from the pump) to exit and begin its path up the wall and out of the house. See **Figure 5**. No gravel should enter the crock!

- Test the clean, finished trench with a softly running garden hose to check the slope of the trench. The water should run quickly to the sump well.

- Pour ¾-inch washed gravel into the bottom of the trench to an even 4 inches deep all the way around the trench area. Naturally, the entry holes into the crock should be adjusted accordingly for the draintile, leaving gravel underneath the draintile.

- Use couplings to join the 10-foot pieces of 4-inch perforated pipe. The flexible draintile will bend around corners, which eliminates the need for all sorts of elbows, 45^0, 90^0, etc.

- Although I recommend solid schedule 40 PVC perforated pipe for new construction, ADS perforated pipe is just fine for this application. No one will step on it since great care is taken and the installers have the entire floor slab to walk on. If the pipe silts up, it must be dug up and the gravel needs to be replaced. The pipe must then be flushed and reinstalled. It cannot be snaked to clear it; the silt cannot be removed in that manner. So, the heavier pipe is unnecessary.

- Step lightly on the pipe after it is laid into the trench and pour gravel onto the pipe. Leave about 2 inches at the top free of gravel. This will allow room for the cement floor you are going to pour. Make sure the gravel is well tamped by foot to remove air spaces.

- Run the discharge line from the pump and out the wall. Run it at least 15' to 20' away from the house. Follow the manufacturer's directions.

- Fill in around the sump well with gravel.

- Double bleed all the cinder blocks as seen in **Figure 11**.

- Install the wall vent plate as seen in **Figure 11**. The gravel has not been depicted for clarity's sake, but the plate rests on the gravel bed that has been spread over the footing. Use a small amount of gravel to hold the plate in place until the cement can be poured. Examine the drawings closely, they will tell you the story much better than I can. The plate must run continuously wherever the system goes. Overlap the pieces of plate by snipping out 1 inch of the bottom lip so that one piece can be hung over the adjacent piece. The overlap will be 1 inch. Corners can be negotiated by using aviation snips to cut a slit in the upper and lower lips of the plate and then bending the plate to a 90^0 angle. The plate can be fabricated at any sheet metal contractor. Ask for 22 gauge hot tin dipped galvanized steel. See **Figure 10** for size specifications.

- Cement the floor back using regular pre-packaged sandmix cement or mix your own using one part of Portland cement to 2 ½ parts of builder's sand. After wetting the floor slab to assure a good bond with the new cement and minimal shrinkage, use a 12-inch finisher's trowel to spread and smooth the cement so that it is even with the exiting slab. A level might be helpful to make sure that your new floor surface doesn't drop down or rise up.

- All debris can be taken to the nearest landfill by pick-up truck or dump truck.

- Once again, do not use an air hammer. These create too much dust!

This blow-by-blow description cannot contain every little step you'll take, nor every situation you'll encounter. However, if you are brave enough to tackle the work in the first place, this "how to" section will provide you with all the basic techniques utilized in the installation of a sub-floor water pressure relief system, combined with a wall drainage and vent system. Practice will build your skills quickly.

EXCAVATION ON EXISTING WALLS

We've considered in depth the techniques I advocate for sealing a newly constructed wall. (See **Figure 3**) I would like to add a few pertinent details, or variations, applicable when digging up an older wall.

First of all, see the illustration in **Figure 13**. This shows a very simple view of the correct versus the incorrect way to dig a deep trench. The dotted line shows a "dig" that will most often end up caving in. Since some of these "digs" can be 8' - 12' in depth, it's safe to say that you don't want to be standing at the bottom of such a trench when it caves in. This could permanently curtail your career as a do-it-yourself waterproofer. If you slope your trench as shown, safety is assured, and you can tell your grandchildren about your below-grade exploits. Enough said?

If there are space limitations and available room will not permit such a wide trench, then consult with an excavation contractor about his digging and shoring up the trench. You can then seal the wall, saving many dollars, and the contractor can backfill for you. This would be a rare occurrence though, since enough room is normally present to allow a wide, sloping, safe trench.

Most older walls will have completely lost their tar coating by the time they are excavated. The cement parging will be in a degraded state, perhaps sandy and cracked. If the tar coating is gone, clean all loose particles of the old parging off of the wall with a wire brush and a hammer. Spray the wall briskly with a jet stream from your garden hose. While the wall is still damp, parge on a new coat of cement at least ½ inch thick. The mix used is one part cement, 1/4 part hydrated lime, and three parts sand. This mix has good workability and high strength. Roughen this coat while it's still wet with a notched trowel.

FIGURE 13 SAFE SLOPE EXCAVATION DETAIL

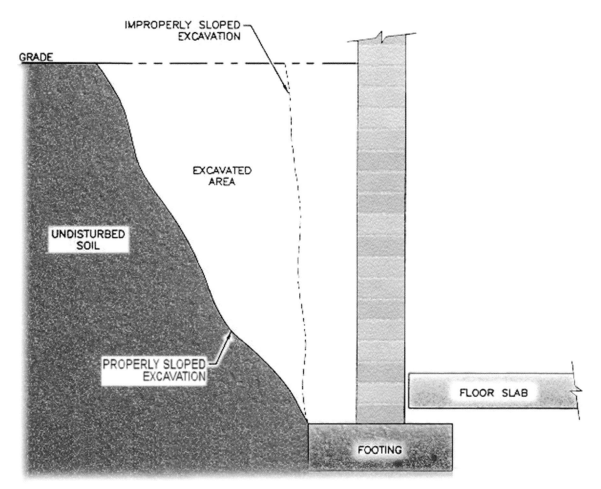

SAFE SLOPE
EXCAVATION DETAIL
NOT TO SCALE

In 24 hours apply a second coat of cement. Smooth this coat of cement to a smooth surface using a steel trowel. This coat should be at least ½ inch thick as well. In two to three days, this wall should be dry and ready for the subsequent sealing process as described in Paragraph 3 of Chapter 2.

Should the wall, however, be relatively young enough in age that it still retains its tar coating, then you need not reparge with cement. Fully clean the excavated wall of all dirt residue. First, dry out all visible cracks with a handheld propane torch and then seal these cracks with a rubberized caulk such as NP1 made by Sonneborn Products. Wait a day and then apply a new coat of plastic asphalt. Finally, proceed on with the subsequent steps as outlined in Paragraphs 3 through 12 of Chapter Two. If an exterior draintile system is required, reread the last four paragraphs of Chapter Two, which covers the correct methods to use. Also, see **Figure 6**. *(Call your local utility company and mark all pipes, wires, etc. before beginning any excavation.)*

MONOLITHIC SLABS

I am very briefly going to mention these unusual but occasionally seen foundations. I've rarely run across these in residential construction, but larger buildings constructed on minimally solid ground, use this foundation type frequently. The monolithic slab is very stable and boasts great strength.

Look at **Figure 14**. You'll note that the floor slab and the footing are one integral piece. They are heavily reinforced with steel bars. The cinder block wall is constructed right on the unit of concrete.

As with other wall types, should severe wall seepage e present, then excavation is in order. What usually happens with this type of foundation configuration is this: water enters the basement where the cinder block meets the floor slab. There is a seam here that falls prey to the inadequate membrane syndrome we've seen so often. Since this type of seepage is minor, not worthy of a full-blown excavation to correct it, a plate system will suffice. This plate system can be vented into a sump pump.

FIGURE 14 MONOLITHIC SLAB WITH PLATE SYSTEM

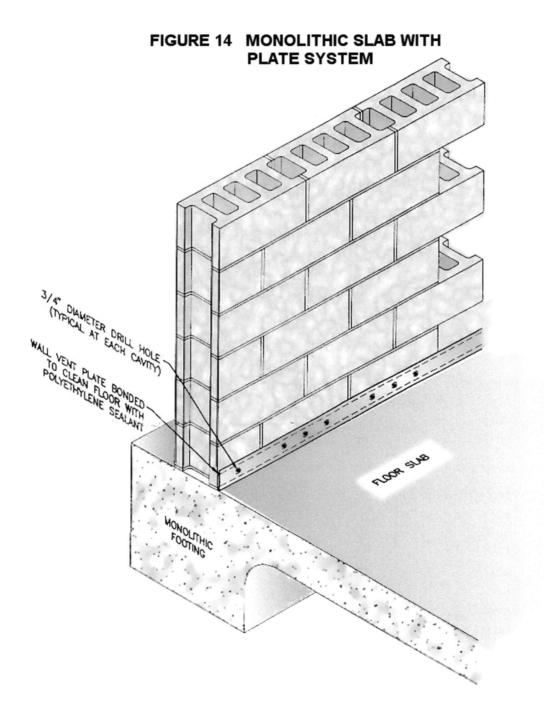

3/4" DIAMETER DRILL HOLE (TYPICAL AT EACH CAVITY)

WALL VENT PLATE BONDED TO CLEAN FLOOR WITH POLYETHYLENE SEALANT

FLOOR SLAB

MONOLITHIC FOOTING

MONOLITHIC SLAB WITH PLATE SYSTEM
NOT TO SCALE

If paneling or Sheetrock is obstructing the installation, it can be removed up to a height of 4 ½ inches using a circular saw and a sawzall. A 1-inch **by** 6-inch baseboard can be used to replace the removed wood. A good carpenter can do a hundred-foot job for around $300.00 to $400.00, if you can't do it yourself.

The plate is bonded directly onto the floor after the cinder blocks have been bled. The floor must be clean, dust-free and dry. Once the plate is laid into place, a bead of NP1, or any good polyurethane caulking, is applied to the base of the plate. Press the bead onto the floor with a plastic spoon, creating a neat, smooth continuous joint. Seal all overlaps between pieces of plate.

When the plate reaches the sump pump, slit the bottom lip and bend it down, parallel with the body of the plate before sealing it to the floor. This will form a channel, holding back the gravel surrounding the sump well. Any water running inside the plate will find the sump pump and the little channel created, then run down into the gravel bed. Cement can be laid right up to the plate now as seen in **Figure 12**. The whole thrust is to create a watertight channel that can carry water to the pump. Once the cement around the pump has cured, which takes about 10 days or so, a bead of caulking can be laid and spooned onto the plate where it meets this new cement, which further enhances the watertight seal. Wherever a plate system terminates, the end of the piece obviously needs to be filled with caulk and sealed. Spoon this joint to make it smooth and neat.

WINDOW WELLS & STAIRWELL DRAINS

In the course of writing this publication, I've zeroed in on the main problem areas associated with basement seepage. Most homeowners are cognizant enough concerning their basement's daily condition, to be aware of the particular areas that regularly show water penetration. Occasionally though, an entire basement receives a thorough waterproofing treatment, be it excavation, interior draintile, or both, simply because of a misdiagnosis. It's kind of like the patient who enters the hospital to have an ingrown toenail removed, and comes out missing a kidney.

My point is that water can enter a basement through window wells and basement stairwell drains, and it can enter in great quantities. Primarily, this occurs when leaf debris or some other kind of organic debris chokes up the normal flow of water. In the case of a window well that regularly builds up water and spills the Water into the basement, the remedy can be simple. I have known of unscrupulous salesmen or contractors taking advantage of the homeowner's ignorance of the situation, and selling them a high-dollar waterproofing system when an hour's worth of work by one person would have sufficed. Be aware of and familiar with the condition of your basement. Try to observe it during heavy rains. Try to catch it leaking!

Back to the window well. First, make sure that there isn't a downspout nearby dumping a large volume of water into the window well. Second, remove all the old gravel in the window well, if there is any, and drop the level of soil by 18 to 24 inches below its present level. Create a larger reservoir. You'll remove a lot of decaying organic matter that has washed or blown into the well and consequently impedes the water's ability to percolate downwards. After lowering the level of the soil inside the well, add a 6 to 8 inch layer of gravel (3/4-inch washed gravel). Third, cover the well with a window well bubble. This will prevent leaf debris, etc. from filling the well again.

If a window well doesn't respond to this modification, it may be necessary to install a sump pump in the well using all the techniques described earlier, but with a much smaller container due to space limitation. Another alternative is this: if there is an interior draintile system, the window well can be drained using a 1¼-inch pipe running through the wall and directly down into the draintile pipe below. If this procedure were pursued, I would strongly suggest installing a backup pump.

Stairwell drains can become inoperative if the drain cover becomes clogged with leaves, grass clippings, twigs, etc. Once again, try to keep large amounts of water from descending the steps of the stairwell as the water can carry with it silt and organic debris. During a heavy rain, observe the water drainage patterns in the yard. Do they affect the stairwell? Try having a professional snake the drain to clear it. The older homes often have only a drywell under the stairwell floor, or a pipe long since broken with rust. Inevitably, these will fail and permit water to flow unabated into the basement. I've installed hundreds, if not thousands, of sump pumps in stairwells to act as a drain. The lid of the container can be drilled with holes to accept water. This may be your only alternative. To keep the discharge line from freezing in such an installation, drill a hole using the smallest drill bit you can find (1/32-inch) into the discharge line just above the check valve. This will let the water drain out of the line, but not quickly enough to exasperate the pump. But, remember the hole must be about the size of a pinhead.

CHAPTER 5

Dampness

Without a doubt, the most subjective of all waterproofing terms is the word "dampness," denoting basement moisture content. Homeowners have widely varying perceptions as to exactly what dampness is.

For example, I have been in basements that were as dry as a desert and yet the homeowner ran a dehumidifier around the clock because he perceived the "cool" air of the basement to be moist. Dehumidifiers, even in the driest of basements, will always find ambient water vapor to condense on their refrigerated coil units.

A dehumidifier takes advantage of the constant natural law that causes water vapor to convert to its liquid form if it is subjected to a sufficient drop in temperature. When water droplets condense on the outside of a cold glass of ice water; or the skin of an ice-cold watermelon drips with condensed water, this natural phenomenon is taking place. A dehumidifier's refrigerated coils cause ambient water vapor coming into contact with them to change into a liquid, which is then collected in a reservoir pan for disposal.

I've been in basements where the complaint was "excessive moisture." The dehumidifier was humming away and the air was so dry it was like breathing in cotton balls. Now, that person was not experiencing a moisture problem in an objective sense, but subjectively, they were convinced they were. This homeowner perceived "coolness," which is inherently present in below grade spaces, as dampness.

On the other hand, I've been in homes where the basement was located on a spring-active subsoil; water was oozing in everywhere and the homeowner characterized the basement as "cool," but not as damp or moist! So after years of dealing with this illusory situation, it's obvious that these perceptions don't always arise out of an accurate interpretation of conditions. Rather, what is at work here is individual sensory cognition. More simply put, it's "different strokes for different folks!"

There is, however, a truth to the matter. There exists an objective, unbiased reality. All basements are cool, but not all basements are moist with seepage. The question is this: how do you accurately judge the difference between cool and moist? When will it be appropriate to spend hard-earned money on corrective procedures and when will it be uncalled for?

If your basement displays:

- mold and mildew on the walls, wall coverings, floor and furnishings;

- water stains on the walls, particularly where the floor meets the walls;

- efflorescence;

- a floor that sweats in spring;

- condensation forming on glassy surfaces during the spring and summer;

- rotted wood products on the floor and wall areas;

- rust on metal objects where they meet the floor or walls,

then your basement shows signs that indicate the presence of water under and around the foundation and calls for remedial action. A dehumidifier will mask the problem to some extent, but will not solve it.

If your basement shows none of these signs and has never leaked, then you can relax. For the time being, you are the possessor of a healthy, dry, strong basement. If you feel more physically comfortable by running your dehumidifier, then by all means, do so.

CHAPTER 6 —————————————

Radon Gas

Radon gas is present in many American basements. Concentrations of the gas vary from locale to locale. This gas is tasteless, odorless, and you can't see it. The bad news is that this gas is also carcinogenic. It will incite cancer.

There are many ways to test for the presence of the gas, from passive-exposure test kits obtained in your local hardware store, to contacting local environmental agencies who can use sophisticated, highly accurate equipment to detect the harmful gas.

If you should test for and detect radon in your home, local environmental agencies can recommend a contractor who will rid your home of the gas. The good news is that interior draintile systems lend themselves well to this process. All wall vent systems and sump wells need to be sealed airtight, but the systems can be easily adapted to help in the fight against radon infiltration of your home.

Testing for the gas is certainly prudent and I encourage it. It is also wise to follow up the generic, over-the-counter test kits with procedures that are more accurate.

CHAPTER 7 ———————————————————

Choosing a Contractor

The choice you make concerning an individual, his company and their collective competence to solve your seepage problems, should not be based solely upon the salesperson's appearance, demeanor, his slick sales pitch, the company's credentials or price quotations. Rather, the preponderance of your decision should be based upon the technical approach the contractor intends to take to correct your problem.

It is very difficult to judge a book by its cover, or so the old saying goes. But a book's contents will surely divulge its intent. I'm not being facetious when I claim that having obtained this publication is a good first step towards discerning the intent of a salesperson or estimator. You must try to educate yourself about your seepage problem and the peculiarities of your basement before the sales "rep" arrives. With this approach, you are in a better position to evaluate his abilities and experience. You'll be more able to determine if the individual is just a salesperson who may next week be selling vinyl siding when he can't master the fundamentals of basement waterproofing sales. Or, is he what he purports to be, an expert who can design a system to solve your problem in an efficient, cost effective way?

If you are not educated in the crucial fundamentals of basement waterproofing, a sales representative can tell you anything and educate you with misinformation. It can be rather like putting a fox in charge of the chicken coop.

I am aware of many so-called waterproofing contractors that are nothing more than a high pressure sales organization that subcontracts out all of its work to private subcontractors. These individuals are independent of the parent organization, but they are the ones who install the job, collect the payment, return the payment to the sales organization and secure payment for their work. The parent organization may or may not have their own in-house service department that performs post-installation service work. It's not unheard of for the parent company to send the original subcontractor back to your home if his work is unsuccessful. This can become a nightmare of never ending service calls. If the crew couldn't solve the problem by using thorough, proven techniques the first time out, what makes anyone believe they can achieve final success through a series of piecemeal attempts?

The pitfalls encountered in this type of setup can be many. I have seen these types of business arrangements yield good results, but rarely. Primarily, though, it is the salesperson who determines what path your installation is going to travel down. Will this individual correctly assess your problem and prescribe the appropriate treatment? Will the work order schematic he hands the crew really get to the heart of the problems afflicting your basement? Or will he sell you a generic procedure that doesn't really offer you a permanent solution to your situation, but does generate lots of cash for the sales organization and himself? How will you know?

What separates the expert from the sales imposter is this: what is the company policy on wall seepage? If you are undergoing severe wall seepage, with water penetrating at various points, both high and low on the wall, what does the estimator say? Does he recommend a floor system and insist on excavating the wall and resealing it using techniques akin to those advocated in this publication? Or does he tell you that a simple interior draintile system will remedy the wall problems? Does he try to discourage excavation on the basis that it is simply too expensive to be considered? The genuine expert will recommend a reasonably priced excavation and floor system. The counterfeit expert will sell you only a floor system, but will charge you enough money to have also installed interior draintile and excavated the wall. Then the sales person and the sales organization will divide the spoils. And you'll get a sub-floor system followed by lots of service calls.

Why is this distinction the acid test? Here's why:

- The interior draintile system can be installed at any future time, regardless of the weather or the time of year, which makes for steady cash flow.

- The interior draintile system can be installed without heavy equipment (backhoes) and experienced operators. It's expensive to keep an in-house crew dedicated to the purpose of excavation. And it is difficult to get reliable excavation subcontractors at short notice. And crews that dig walls by hand burnout fast without constant attention.

- The floor system adapts well to a canned sales pitch that can be learned and recited by anyone.

- Unlike excavation combined with floor systems, a simple floor system has a fixed cost and therefore doesn't require a true expert to estimate cost. The problem is that companies specializing only in interior draintile systems will collect their payment after installation, hoping that the wall seepage will respond. When it doesn't, they will send back a one-man service crew to apply an interior wall sealant, generally with a paintbrush. This is not what you paid your money for!

- The draintile system (interior) certainly has an important place in the toolbox of techniques at the disposal of the experienced, honest contractor. But there is a much larger profit margin if excavation is supplanted by interior sealants, which typically have a short, ineffective lifespan. An honest contractor can install an interior system, excavate problem areas and still stay very competitive in price. That's the individual you need to find.

If you can find a contractor who prescribes the proper techniques to keep your basement dry and you feel confident in the individual's ability and honesty, then price comes into play. A fair price for an interior draintile system with a wall ventilation system included should run about $45.00 to $50.00 per linear foot. The pump set-up may run about $600.00. Excavation should run about $150.00 to $200.00 per linear foot, depending upon the depth of the footing. This would, of course, include sealing the wall, backfilling, etc. Sorry, no re-landscaping!

If the estimator wants to charge you over $7000.00 for an average 100 foot interior draintile system that calls for one or two pumps, he's gouging you. Sure, the estimator will justify the extra price by touting the company's 20 year or even lifetime guarantee. But if the job is done thoroughly the first time out, how much service work should be necessary? And I can count the companies that have truly been around for 20 years on my hands! I don't care if the Prince of Wales is going to install the job in a Mercedes dump truck, $7,000.00 for such a contract is too much...shop around!

Always get three or more estimates. More would be preferable. The high-pressure salesperson will simply need to await your reply to his quotation. And make no mistake, all estimators will want you to sign a contract the night they are there in your living room. There will be inducements to sign. These come-ons generally appear in the form of price "drops" or limited-time-only discounts. The larger the price drops, the less trustworthy the individual is. Whenever I quoted a price for a job, I gave only one figure. Take it or leave it. I didn't expect to wrestle the prospective customer out of his or her desire to shop around. I would, though, generally hear back later from the individual that they wanted to go with my proposal. Expertise and fair pricing win out in the end, most times.

Always, but always, check with the Better Business Bureau and the Home Improvement Commission in your area to research a contractor's complaint record. Call the Attorney General's office in your state. Call the Federal Bankruptcy Court in the area where the company is located. Companies can file for Chapter 11 bankruptcy and still keep their doors open for business. And they aren't required to disclose any financial information to anyone, least of all you.

Ask how long the company has been at its current address. Visit the office if you can. Visit a job in progress, if possible. Talk to the crewmembers. Do they have good attitudes? Are they neat and clean? Is their equipment in good condition? Are their vehicles well maintained? Do they take pride in their work? These are all-important considerations. Truly, pictures are worth a thousand words. Give your intuition a chance to work.

My ideal contractor would fit this profile:

- The salesperson or estimator would be the owner or co-owner of a small, stable outfit. He is very knowledgeable, having been in business for 10 years or more. His company can boast an excellent record with very few or no complaints. His word-of-mouth reputation is excellent.

- He gives an informative presentation of the techniques he employs. These techniques include excavation, when necessary, and at a fair price. In fact, he'll advocate excavation to avoid future service problems that can detrimental to both you and himself.

- His office is neat and small, unencumbered by a high overhead. He doesn't drive an overtly expensive, ostentatious automobile. He's conservative.

- His working staff, crew chiefs and laborers are well motivated with good attitudes.

- His prices are in line with recommendations put forth in this publication.

- He doesn't advertise incessantly or pay for a huge Yellow Pages ad, since from the customer's point of view, the less overhead, the better. Can you guess who pays for the overhead?

- He'll gladly wait for you to secure three estimates, and while mildly aggressive, won't try to pressure you into signing the first night.

Look for someone who fits this profile as closely as possible, and you'll have a winner.

WHEN THE UNTHINKABLE HAPPENS

If you have obtained this publication after work was done in your home and the work was unsatisfactory, here are some suggestions.

If you have paid for the work and the company isn't cooperating with your appeals for service, or the service work isn't achieving hard results, you should:

- Keep track of and document names and dates. Keep a record of all interaction, telephone calls, etc., and what was said or promised.

- Take pictures of leaking areas for future reference.

- If satisfaction isn't forthcoming, send a certified letter to the president of the company. Request a return receipt. Outline the problems you have encountered. Also, send copies to the Better Business. Bureau, the Home Improvement

Commission and the Attorney General's Office.

- Don't call a lawyer yet. This may be an unnecessary expense. The agencies listed above can have plenty of clout and can force the company in question to rectify any and all problems.

- Obtain a copy of "The Consumer's Resource Handbook" from the Consumer Information Center in Pueblo, Colorado 81009. This book contains a nationwide listing of local, city, county and state consumer groups that may also be able to help you.

- Make all complaints formal and in writing.

I sincerely hope that this publication has fulfilled its goal. I trust that I've helped put you on the road leading towards an economical, long lasting restoration of your basement to a fresh, dry and enjoyable part of your home.

13031974R00053

Made in the USA
Lexington, KY
13 January 2012